Under My Skin

Omar "Crispy" Avila

Omar "Crispy" Avila

ISBN: 978-1-7367872-5-0

DEDICATION

I would like first to thank my mom and dad. You've been more than a blessing throughout my life and continue to be today. You have motivated me to keep going and have always stood by my side, guiding and walking with me on this life journey, teaching and shaping me into the man I am. And to my brother and sister, I want to thank you for always having my back. More than you'll ever know. The two of you have shown me love and support, no matter what, and I can never thank you enough for that. To my nieces and nephews, who continue to be my biggest fans and supporters. My niece Haley, you will forever be my beacon of light and ray of sunshine. You've impacted my life in ways I could never repay. I would also like to thank my buddies Rick, David, Chris, and Jay, also wounded in action. Also, to the thousands of you who have supported me over the years. Those who take their time to listen or read about my story. I wouldn't be here if it weren't for your love and support. Last but certainly not least, I would like to thank my loving and always caring wife. The one who's continuously pushing me forward and encouraging me to be better each day. I love you and can't wait to see what the future has in store for us.

Omar "Crispy" Avila

CONTENTS

Omar "Crispy" Avila

Omar "Crispy" Avila

IT'S PARTY TIME

*P*arty. That simple, five-letter word can encompass unforgettable memories that last a lifetime. When I reflect on some of the parties I've had during my time on earth thus far, the energy felt among friends and loved ones stand out the most. I may not recall all that was said or each name in attendance, but I'll never forget the spiritual energy shared. This five-letter word, as described in the dictionary, is a noun. It's a term that represents an event or social gathering. Often involving entertainment and celebration among invited guests.

A party is something that many of us have had a chance to experience in some way, shape, or form. Regardless of age, culture, or origin, parties are an event everyone can relate to. It's like a phenomenon that links us together, similar to music. However, the word *party* had a completely different meaning for me at a particular time as a young child living in Villahermosa, Tabasco, Mexico. Back then, it was what could potentially prevent us from having a better livelihood for my family. Or worse, face dire consequences.

I was a young child during that time growing up in Mexico. I couldn't have been more than five or six years old. I lived in a small town near the capital of Tabasco in southern Mexico before my family settled in a small apartment in Tamaulipas. Mexico is where I was born. It's the place and home where my origins began, and I spent a portion of my childhood. After meeting and marrying my mother, Patricia, after a couple of months of dating, my dad, Guillermo, moved to

Mexico, where she lived. They met while my dad was touring in his band. After his four-year enlistment, serving as a tanker, he decided to create a band that traveled around the United States and Mexico, performing in numerous cities and towns.

My dad always wanted the best for his family, myself, and my two younger siblings, my brother and sister. So, he often worked local, small-time labor jobs in Mexico while my mother worked at a farmers' market owned by my grandfather. My parents weren't around often, so it was my job, as the oldest, to care for my siblings and me. My dad often spent most of his time working to make ends meet during the work week. From sun up to sun down, Monday through Friday.

He was tired and drained from the exhaustive work when he came home. But, regardless of how tired he was, he made time for us. Always ensuring he could bring a smile to all of our faces, no matter how he may have felt. That's the man my dad was and continues to be today. He is a hard worker that will do whatever it takes to provide for his family.

Mexico, from what I can remember, in the late eighties and early nineties, was a lot different from what we see on the news today. While crime and poverty existed in Mexico when I was a kid, it wasn't as bad of a situation as it is now. Well, that's at least how I saw it. Instead, Mexico was a vibrant country full of life and history. In my community, the neighbors were friendly and cared for one another. They'd look after each other's kids while we played outside. And if you ever needed anything, there seemed always to be a friendly neighbor to help.

"Party." In English, my dad said to me. A rare occurrence in a household where Spanish is mostly spoken. He pronounced the word looking sternly at me. The look two adult men would give one another, conversing seriously and meaningfully. A look that I hadn't seen before in his eyes.

It was a Sunday afternoon. A day that I find myself from time to time reminiscing. My mom was in her final stages of wrapping up a meal for my brother, sister, and me in the kitchen. Her home-cooked Sunday meals produced an aroma more vivid than memories themselves. Authentic Mexican dishes, with ingredients only a mother has mastered from years of trial and error, passed down from generation to generation.

My dad frantically burst through our apartment door, carrying a handful of new clothes and brightly colored and decorated balloons.

"What's going on, Guillermo?" My mother asked.

"Nothing, sweetheart. We're going to a party!" He replied.

"A party, Guillermo? What party are you talking about?"

"I'll explain a little later. But for right now, I need you to get dressed and grab whatever you can. While you do that, I'll get the kids ready to go." He replied while passing out a few of the balloons to us kids.

As confused as we were, we listened to my dad's instructions. While my mom was getting dressed and washing up, my dad dressed my brother, sister, and me in the new clothing he carried. He didn't say much, from what I remember. Instead, he moved at what seemed to be light speed as he dressed the three of us, repeating the same word slowly. "Party."

I assumed because I was the oldest, is why he was paying so much attention to me. Reciting the word over and over. He wanted me to remember the word and repeat it to myself until it was ingrained into my brain. To the point that when I was to say it out loud, I spoke it without hesitation and confidence. My dad also clarified that I needed to learn it quickly, as time was unfortunately not on our side.

Before my mom could finish getting dressed and grabbing what she could, my dad and the rest of us piled into his car. A Chrysler Lebaron convertible. Manufactured during the eighties, the Lebaron bolstered an automatic four-speed in a three-liter, V-6 engine. Unfortunately, it wasn't the best and most comfortable means of transportation either.

"Don't forget the English word. I want you to remember Omar." My dad said to me once more, looking back over his shoulder as he sat in the driver's seat.

After a brief wait, my mom finally made her way out of the apartment and joined the rest of us. The look on her face was what I guess you could expect, especially given the circumstances. Other than my dad, none of us knew what was going on or where we were heading. However, considering the gifts and new clothes, wherever we were going, I thought it would at least be worth the spur-of-the-moment trip. Besides, it wasn't often that we took trips as a family together.

We drove for what seemed like hours. My brother and sister would fade in and out of sleep—alternating sleeping on each other's shoulders. I managed to grab a few minutes of shut-eye myself, even for a few brief moments. The only thing that prevented me from staying asleep had been the anticipation of where we were heading. As well as the sound of my dad's voice in my head, repeating the English word I learned before leaving.

My dad, however, showed no signs of fatigue, despite a long day's work. On the contrary, he seemed as focused and keen on the road as ever. Not saying much of anything and minimizing distractions by not playing music over the car's radio. My mother, on the other hand, remained all but silent. Sitting in the passenger seat, my mom's focus was out of her side window. As I sat behind her, I could hear her mumbling in a soft tone under her breath. Whatever she was saying, I noticed that she had been doing so since we left.

It took me some time, but I eventually realized she was reciting one of her favorite prayers.

"May the Lord Jesus Christ be with me. That he may defend me; may He be within me, that He may conserve me; may He be before me that He may lead me. May He be after me, that He may guard me. Above me, that He may bless me, who with God the Father and the Holy Spirit and reigns forever and ever. Amen."

My mother's faith and strong beliefs are why

I consider her one of the strongest, most precious women on earth. And our religious upbringing is what I believe to be the backbone and the mold that continues to hold our family together.

The ride, for the most part, was an uneventful one. There wasn't anything that seemed to catch my eye or cause much of an alarm. The sun was starting to set, and I wasn't sure how long I could remain seated, crammed in the back of my dad's car. And by now, my rear end was growing numb with each mile that passed.

"Look over there. The bridge." My dad perked up in his seat, grabbed the steering wheel with both hands, and said aloud.

Sitting upright, trying to peer over the dashboard, I could see what my dad was referring to. In the distance, a well-kept, wide, multi-lane bridge stood above and intersected smaller roads beneath. While I had seen bridges before, I had never seen one like the one we were about to cross. This one looked as if it stretched and extended into the distance into the horizon, as far as I could see.

I guess this means that we're almost there! I thought. It would be the only reason my dad seemed enthusiastic about seeing it.

"How are you, sir? May I ask your reasoning for entering the United States." A man dressed in a matching olive drab button-up shirt and pants asked my dad while peering into the driver's window.

"I'm doing well. I'm taking my family to their cousin's birthday party at a Mcdonald's in Brownsville." He responded. His English was what I assumed to be perfect. And the first time that I heard my dad carry on a conversation in a language other than Spanish.

"Is that right young man? Do you know where you are going?" The unknown man then looked passed my dad and asked me.

I didn't know what any of the words he was saying to me meant. The words coming out of his mouth could have been anything, and I wouldn't have had the slightest clue. Although, there was one word that stood out clearly to me. So, without hesitation, I quickly regurgitated what my dad taught me to say before leaving.

"Party!" I replied with the confidence that only a child could display, knowing it would make my parents proud.

"Well! You make sure you have fun at the party, young man." He responded. The both of us exchanged a friendly smile and a wave. Still, I was completely oblivious to what was said to me or what was happening. However, there was one thing for certain; I said the word. At that moment, that was all that I cared about.

My dad gave me an important task only a big brother could accomplish, and I knocked it out of the park. I could tell that my dad was more than pleased with me. While he didn't say it verbally, the look that he had, looking back at me in his rearview mirror, was worth more than words he could have offered. Meanwhile, my mom stayed in her prayer. Reciting it over and over to herself, still unsure what my dad was up to. I guess that's all that she felt that she could do. But, it seemed to be the only thing bringing her peace in light of everything going on.

At the drop of a hat and, for several unknown reasons, my dad decided that day that it was time for us to move. A choice that had the potential of not going as smoothly as it had. Or how my dad planned it out in his mind as we crossed over into the United States of America, where we would stay. We left most of what we had behind in Mexico, carrying the few items that could fit into a convertible and the clothes we wore on our backs.

I wouldn't understand until sometime after what had taken place. The English word, party, and what it meant and how the events would impact my life forever. We were on a one-way trip to a new land. A new place full of opportunities and a better life. A new home where we would have to start from scratch and had the potential for a brighter future for the five of us. That's if we played our cards right.

My dad's belief that we would make it into

the states was something he regarded as fact. But, there wasn't a doubt in his mind that things wouldn't work out. So, sometime before crossing the border, my dad was busy planning. He was able to rent out a one-bedroom house in Brownsville, where we would all live. A small and cramped home that I'm still amazed that we all managed to fit without going after each other's heads. Our sleeping arrangements weren't always the most pleasant with only one bedroom as you'd imagine. My sister and brother slept on the bed with my mom. My bed was the comfortable sofa in our living room with my dad sleeping on the hard floor beneath me. While it sucked at times, it's what we had to do as a family for that year until our finances were better and we could afford a better place.

Moving to the states meant that we'd not only have to adapt quickly. It also meant learning a new language and meeting new people. Understanding the customs and its traditions and how we could contribute. Everything it took involved America being the greatest country on the planet. Tasks that may not be at first easy to grasp and understand, especially at a young age. But they were necessary if we wanted to survive and thrive.

My family settled not too far from the US, Mexico border in Brownsville. It is a small town in the south Texas city, with San Antonio being its neighbor, two hundred and seventy-seven miles away. At the time, Brownsville's population was just over one hundred thousand. The community where we lived was often quiet, similar to the city itself. Its serenity and welcoming people were what it was known for. Everyone kept to themselves, and for the most part, everyone knew one another. I suppose this had to do with the fact that much of Brownsville's population arrived in the city just as my family had. Illegally.

Brownsville is a known settling spot for many individuals and families seeking refuge and to start a better life in the United States. A distance of fewer than five miles from the border. Around a ten-minute drive in a car. And, it was a little less than an hour's walk for those who decided to take their chances and evade the border patrol on foot. Considering the circumstances and conditions you may encounter while living in Mexico, this journey was well worth the risk for some.

After spending some time in Brownsville, my siblings and I were able to become enrolled in school. I attended one of the area's local elementary and middle schools while my dad continued to work. His work wasn't much different from what he did in Mexico, although it was stable. He worked as Sous-chef at a restaurant in South Padre Island, Texas. His job as a Sous-chef was to serve under the main chef, operating as second in command in the kitchen and primarily prepping the food and organizing the meals prepared by the chef.

On the other hand, my mom worked the shrimp fields in knee-deep mud in Lower Rio Grande, Texas, known as the Valley. Her job was picking shrimp in the fields, paid by the bucket, to be sold to local seafood markets. As for myself, contributing what I could, I took the responsibility of looking after the family while my parents worked.

I didn't find adjusting to the states as difficult as some would assume. Instead, I found the experience to be rather exciting. While in school, I learned my second language, English, and met new friends. The ease of my transition is credited to the classes and the teachers who taught at my school. It was somewhat of a foreign student classroom experience. A classroom primarily composed of kids in the same situation as me. We are forced to learn, comprehend, and communicate in an environment much different than we came from.

A lot changed for my family and me. Years had flown by in what felt like a blink of an eye, and before I could realize it, I was in high school. I was sixteen years old, standing six feet, two inches tall, and coming in at one-hundred and eighty-five pounds. Far from your average teen in his sophomore year, to say the least. I also had a very promising career in football, with nothing more than the hopes to take my skills to the next level.

Perhaps at some prominent college in a nice state, before trying my luck at making it at the professional level.

It would be a dream come true. Graduating college, playing football in the pros, and providing for my family for once would mean everything. Statistically, though, I knew the odds were stacked against me, and my chances were slim. But, after all that it took for us to get here and make way for ourselves and the overwhelming odds we had to face, I knew nothing was out of my reach. It all seemed to fall into place, and our lives were all coming together.

My family's future in America continued to get brighter. Especially during the late summer of 2001. It's a time in my life that I'll never forget, and I continue to cherish the memory today. The date was August 17, 2001. I remember my mom going through the mail while sitting at the dining room table. After grabbing one letter, in particular, she pushed herself away from the table and stood up, holding it close to her chest.

"Everyone, come in here!" She shouted. Her eyes were as big as saucepans and full of excitement.

"What's going on, mom?" I asked, unsure of what was going on.

"It's here! Finally. It's here." She replied.

Even without her telling me exactly what it was, I knew what she was so excited about. In her hands was an official letter from the US government. Inside was a notice for our Naturalization Oath Ceremony. It was the last step my family had to take to officially be citizens of the United States of America. The wait was finally over. After filling out a citizen application and meeting strict requirements, we could finally attend an official citizenship ceremony.

The Naturalization Oath Ceremony is a tradition that dates back to the eighteenth century. A rather long ceremony, somewhere taking between two to three hours. Individuals who were accepted and invited, born worldwide, are asked to take an Oath of Allegiance during the event. An oath to support, defend and protect the US constitution and laws against all enemies. As well as giving up any allegiance to a foreign country or nation and noble titles one may have previously held. The Oath also states that each individual will provide military or civilian services when or if called upon by the United States government.

After taking the Oath, we were then given our Certification of Naturalization. Officially granting us the right to call ourselves and be legally considered American citizens. Until then, it was single-handedly the most pride I had ever felt. I could only imagine what my mom and the rest of my family were experiencing emotionally. As for my dad, I knew that there had to be tons of emotion running through him. Everything from relief to a sense of overwhelming accomplishment and gratifying pride.

My dad took a big and even greater risk of moving my family out of Mexico. Having it pay off, after a long and risky wait, had to have meant the world to him. My dad only wanted the best for us and our future. Now that we were US citizens, he understood, as we all did, that our opportunities were nearly endless.

To think this all began with an off-the-cuff journey and a dream. And the overall success was based on a simple four-letter English word I was forced to learn. I guess you could say that now, the party had officially begun, and we could take pride in celebrating in the greatest nation. The land of the free and the home of the brave. The United States of America.

PAYBACK

*L*iving in Texas came with great pride. Especially now that I was a US citizen. Watching football games on television on the weekends, before each game when the national anthem is played, always affected me differently. To me, it encompassed what it meant to be an American. It represented those who had to sacrifice so much to make this the land it is today. Also, shedding light on all the individuals, regardless of their background, making it the country it is.

This country's hard-working people make it one of the greatest. Those who get up before sunrise work until sunset to provide for their family. The moms and dads who drop their kids off at school every morning so they can go to work. Startup companies and farmers who provide services and goods to their communities. Those who teach the future generations to never give up on their dreams, regardless of what the naysayers believe. In this great big melting pot of a nation, it was hard not to be proud or prideful to be amongst the mix.

Still in high school, about to finish my sophomore year, my dreams of college and football remained a likely possibility. I was playing at the varsity level and was already getting a few looks from potential college scouts. Going off to college, I would be the first to do so. I had every intention of attending. I knew that having a college diploma would mean countless opportunities. And lead to even more doors of possibilities. However, as for many of us during that year in 2001, our future plans would take drastic alternative routes.

September 11, 2001. I was sitting in my

history class when our school's intercom crackled over the speakers.

"Announcement, announcement! If you can do so, teachers and staff are asked to turn on your televisions." The principal of our school announced in an anxious tone.

From the announcement, we all knew that something was wrong. We wouldn't often watch TV while class was in session. Besides its use of watching a boring film, the classroom televisions were rarely on. However, once we saw what was happening on the screen, it wouldn't take long to understand what was happening. Each student and school staff member watched the events of September 11 unfold in front of our eyes.

During this time of year, preparing for the upcoming competitive football season, the school was usually filled with excitement. The graduating seniors who played had high hopes of being noticed for a sports college scholarship. Those who didn't play sports were heading off to college to start the beginning of their adult lives. The excitement was almost palatable and could be heard throughout the halls. Our classroom lessons became fun and relaxed, unlike the schoolwork leading up to a big test.

Today, however, tuning into the news station, the school echoed an eerie silence. It was a day I can recall as if it were yesterday. Like most of us, I knew what I was doing and thinking, where I was, and each emotion that ran through me. Watching the television, the first image I was struck with was the burning tower of the World Trade Center. As I watched, I initially thought about how a pilot could have made such a grave mistake. Thinking of all the lives lost at this moment.

The news coverage continued to play, and the tower continued to billow a large, dark cloud of smoke from its side. My entire classroom sat in complete silence as we watched. Our history teacher stood close to the television at the front of the room. He never moved from his stance, like a stone statue that looked like he had fallen into a trance. Then, a bright red ball of fire exploded outward from the side of the second tower. A second plane, like the first, had struck the building.

"This is intentional." My teacher, Mr. Lopez, said aloud, who still maintained his statuelike appearance.

He was the only person to have said anything since watching the news. Mr. Lopez's words were also the most logical. The likelihood of two pilots of major airliners making the same mistake minutes apart was impossible. This wasn't the cause of some pilot's mistake or of the hands of someone who lacked experience. No. This had to be a deliberate attack. An attack that none of us could fully comprehend of this magnitude.

I gripped the sides of my desk with both hands and squeezed as tight as I could. My grasp was to the point that it started to shake. A state of shock and rage mixed and coursed through me. Watching pieces of paper and the shimmering glass fragments reflecting the sunlight littered the New York streets below. *Who would want to do something like this?* I thought to myself. A country that I found to be one of the best, full of its amazing people, be under attack from someone full of such hate?

My heart felt like it was sinking into the ocean's deepest depths before being crushed by its unimaginable pressure. As the two towers continued to burn ablaze, I remember seeing workers stack into open windows, crying for help as thick smoke swelled behind them. Innocent people who did nothing other than show up to work, or get on a plane, were instantly faced with an unthinkable terror. This was the first time I had witnessed anything like what was happening to the Twin Towers.

"Wait. What is that? Are those people jumping from the tower?" One of my classmates sitting closer to the television asked.

"Yes." Mr. Lopez simply stated. He was monotone and shocked in his response. Although, I could tell he was trying his best to hold back the tremble in his throat as he fought back the tears.

By now, my emotions of shock and rage were met with fear, panic, and sadness. It became so unbearable to keep what I felt inside that I began to cry. I had never traveled to New York and was over a thousand miles away. But, at that moment, I felt as close as ever. It was as if I was watching the horror and terror from the streets of New York.

As tears continued to flow down the sides of my cheek, watching the people fall from the towers, leaping to their death, I was stricken with rage. It was a rage that I had never experienced before. I was usually a calm guy. The most aggressive I ever was, was on the yard lines of a football field, hitting and tackling. However, this rage was much more than I felt during an intense Friday Night Lights match between two rival teams. This rage had violence and revenge fueling it.

I couldn't help but think about what those must have felt on the planes and trapped inside the burning towers. Those who came to a conclusion to leap rather than burn alive shook me to my core. We were witnessing our country being attacked, and at the time, we had no clue who was behind it or what was next. Looking back at the events of

September 11, I find it ironic that I witnessed them while in history class.

We all remained silent with our eyes glued to the television screen. I could hear a few of my classmates sobbing from behind me. We listened to the news reporters give their best idea of what was happening, although the reports changed every few minutes. Then, around 9:30am the lead news anchor announced under a breaking news banner that another attack had occurred. Only this time, near Washington D.C.

"This doesn't make any sense. Who would want to attack us like this?" Mr. Lopez said aloud.

As the news continued to air, we learned that another plane had hit the Pentagon. Our nation's symbol of military strength and influence. America was under a full-fledged attack. Each plane crashed into apparent strategic and pre-determined targets.

The United States is my home. It's the place that has accepted me and provided my family with everything. So witnessing my country under attack was like having a dagger thrust into my heart. Our country represents life and strength to hundreds of millions of people. Seeing it in such a fragile, weak, and shocked state was something I had difficulty wrapping my head around.

Then, at approximately 10:00, around thirty minutes after the Pentagon was hit, we witnessed the impossible. Or at least impossible, was the best I could interpret what was happening at the moment. Thick, light-colored smoke engulfed the upper portion of one of the towers, unlike how it had before, and blew away in the wind current.

The top of the building, which stood over one thousand feet in the air, appeared as if it was sinking into itself. It was like the tower devoured itself from below in a huge plume of smoke, fire, and debris that blew outward. The building continued to shrink downward violently, accompanied by a loud roar.

"No! No! No!" Mr. Lopez shouted from behind his hands, covering his face.

Half of the classroom gasped in shock as if

what we saw had taken their breath away. The tall, shimmering tower had been reduced to rubble within a few seconds. Onlookers on the below streets had to immediately flee and get out of harm's way. Those who survived falling debris were chased through the crowded New York streets by a blinding cloud of smoke that looked like something out of an end-of-the-world movie.

Watching the tower fall was a hard concept to initially grasp. Regardless of what my eyes were showing me, I still found it hard to believe. Or want to consider. Hundreds, if not thousands, of lives were gone in the blink of an eye. Mothers, fathers, sisters, and brothers. Husbands and wives. All people who mattered significantly and were loved by many others, were now dead.

I had yet to let go from the sides of my desk. By now, my knuckles had turned white, and my hands felt as if they were going numb. I remember finding it hard not to think about the events that took place on December 7, 1941. When the Japanese conducted a strikingly similar style attack on naval vessels docked at Pearl Harbor. Innocent people, who chose nothing other than to be where they needed to be and did their job, lost their lives in sudden tragedy.

I couldn't help but imagine how significant what was happening on this day, September 11, and how it would be an event none of us would forget. I understood that everyone that day witnessed a sad piece of history that would be discussed by future generations. For decades, if not longer, long after the dust had settled in the streets of New York.

The morning continued to get worse as the news rolled in. School, for us, had essentially stopped. No bells rang to signify the end of a class and the transition to another. And announcements over the intercom went silent. We were witnessing a pivotal point in our country. A moment in which only one thing mattered or made any sense. And that was to somehow try to understand and comprehend what was happening and be there for each other.

For the first time I recall, America stood in

unison with one another. Regardless of a person's creed, religion, ethnic background, or where they were born, they all share one heart. The heartbeat that keeps America alive and why I consider it great. Sure, it has flaws and a history that cannot be forgotten or overlooked. But what nation doesn't? None of us can stand on our own two feet in perfection in this game that we call life. We're all subject and fallen victim to sin.

Shown on the screen, survivors and witnesses of the collapse consoled one another, gathering in the middle of the street. Those who could help, in any capacity, did what they could. Even if a hug was all that they could offer. The planes that continued to fly in the airspace above our country were forced to land. All air traffic had been grounded for the first time in American history. Besides a few fighter jets that flew above the capital of our nation. They were given specific orders to shoot down any planes over their airspace

However, the horrors of that day were far from over. Everything was happening so fast and unexpectedly. We didn't have a clue as to what the next target was or when it would happen. Then, around 10:30, the second tower collapsed. Similar to the first, crumbling down from its highest portion and onto the streets below. And again, sending a thick, doomsday-like cloud of smoke down the city blocks and streets below. The World Trade Center, an iconic symbol in our country that stood tall amongst the Big Apple skyline, had fallen. Within a short period, a significant blow had been dealt to the core of our nation. What took years to build, admired and sought after by millions, was reduced to ash in a matter of seconds.

I sat in shock and awe, feeling distraught, livid, scared, and furious, all wrapped into a tight ball of emotion. Our history teacher, Mr. Lopez, hunched over with his hands grasping his knees. No longer holding back the tears he had tried fighting back earlier. And rightfully so. I'm sure he could imagine an event like today throughout his years as a history teacher.

Since living in Texas, this was the most

vulnerable I felt. Not knowing when or where the next attack would come from. I could only imagine how those must have felt and what they were experiencing in New York. But, there was one thing that I knew for certain. I had to do something. Even if I knew there wasn't anything I could do to help at the moment.

Then it dawned on me. An idea that I had never taken into consideration before the events of September 11th took place. Right then and there, I decided that I would somehow contribute to our nation. The rage that continued to boil inside made me conclude that I would join the United States armed forces. Hopefully, after graduating, I will somehow get revenge on those attacking us.

I had never thought of joining the military in the past. My goals seemed to be set in stone. The path I had in place had only been to play football. There was no other option or backup plan if things didn't work out the way I dreamed. So, sports was my only outlet to venture off and into a more promising way of life.

While my dad served in the army, joining myself had never crossed my mind. He never talked much about what he did. Other than his job involved driving tanks and some of the good friends that he met during his four-year career. He never said anything bad about serving our country or showed any disdain. Besides seeing a few old pictures and his Army dress uniform, my dad's time in service was rarely a topic he chose to share.

The military lifestyle was foreign to me. I've seen the "Be all you can be" and gungho commercials that aired occasionally or on a Sunday football broadcast. But, I've never paid much attention too much to them, nor did I consider the option to join. The thirty-second ads were nothing more than time fillers or an opportunity to take a breather from an exciting game.

Serving in the armed forces was a guaranteed slot for me to give back. It was the least I could do after seeing the towers fall and the lives lost on that tragic day. I wanted to have the opportunity to be able to provide my services, as a competent body, to my country. After all, I was grateful for a country that had already given so much to my family and me. Regardless of what I thought my future would have been, I knew I was making a decision for all the right reasons. The United States signed a blank check for my family and me that provided us with endless opportunities. I felt that it was my obligation to do the same. By following through and joining the military, I knew that the check I would be signing could cost me my life.

After September 11, America went through various stages of grief, shock, and sadness. Soon after, America would send in its heavy hitters from all branches of the armed forces to redeem the payback the majority of the country wanted. My tenure in high school continued as well, all the while never allowing myself to forget the acts of terror that hit our homeland.

I continued playing football as well. Continuing to shine and be a competitor in a sport I loved with a bright future ahead of me. However,

I knew that I had made myself and my country a promise. A promise that I knew I couldn't allow myself to turn back on. So, during my senior year, I was faced with two ultimate decisions that I had to make. With the school year around the corner and graduation quickly approaching, time was of the essence.

While some of my friends and classmates planned and talked about colleges they would be attending, my mind remained focussed on what I told myself back in 2001. I'll never forget the day I was sitting in the school locker room, taking off football gear and equipment, when I decided. I was going to join the United States Army as an infantryman. That was my sure-shot chance at getting some payback, and the infantry did just that. These were the soldiers facing terrorists, wherever they flourished. And destroyed them.

It wouldn't have sat right with me if I had done anything else. I would have beat myself up for the rest of my life if I went on to try my hand at sports. Seeing news reports of what our brave men and women were doing for the two years I was in school, in some ways, I felt left out. I knew that these soldiers, taking the fight to the enemy, were doing so of their own free will. They made a decision to serve and fight for something greater than themselves. Regardless of what promising future they had planned before enlisting.

Later that evening, after school, I told my mom and dad what I decided to do. While shocked and somewhat saddened, my mom and dad were understanding. They knew the kind of young man I was destined to and had become. During my childhood, my siblings and friends saw me as their protector. Due to my physical size and attributes, it was almost in my nature. However, instead of using my size to bully the little guys, I used it for the opposite. I was someone who would put their body in front of someone else's to take the brunt of the force.

The infantry was where I knew I needed to be. It was the only way I felt I could ensure that what happened on September 11th would never happen again. I understood the dangers of what occurred on the frontlines of the battlefield. I knew there were dangers in a hellish environment that I couldn't begin to fathom unless I saw them for myself. And there was also the possibility that I may never return the same. Or return at all.

The likelihood of me seeing combat was almost certain. Since invading Afghanistan and Iraq, troops have been in heavy contact with the enemy for the past two years. The Taliban and Al Qaeda, the terrorist organizations behind the attacks on US soil, were putting up fierce resistance against our invading forces. Shortly after receiving my high school diploma, that same year in 2004, the Fallujah battle took place. A joint offensive operation led by the United States into the heart of Iraq and terrorist safe haven.

While the enemy forces in Iraq's city of Fallujah were largely destroyed, coalition forces also suffered a blow. According to news reports, it was estimated that over three thousand enemy fighters were either killed or captured. However, one hundred and ten coalition soldiers lost their lives, and five times more were wounded in the battle.

The war in Afghanistan was raging on as well, with few signs that the fighting was near to ending. Moreover, Afghanistan was the suspected and last known location of Osama Bin Laden, the mastermind behind the terrorist attack. So, the enemy putting up most of its resistance here was what you would expect. The last thing our enemy wanted was for us to kill their number one guy. The one who managed to pull off such heinous acts since Pearl Harbor. They would do everything possible, fighting their assess off to defeat the world's superpower.

Considering all things possible, I knew that joining the army was where I needed to be. And while football was no longer in my future, that didn't mean that wouldn't prevent some of my dreams from coming true. By serving in the military, I knew that I was continuing a path where I was able to provide a better life for my family.

Fighting for what I believe in and what

America stands for. To never allow someone to create acts of terror on the innocent again. Not only for my family but for future generations and families all over the country. In addition, I would have my shot at making those bastards pay for what they did to our country. To me, the satisfaction I found in knowing this was something no college or pro sports could offer.

DRESS RIGHT, DRESS!

All it took was my signature on the dotted line. That next year, in 2005, I became a member of the United States armed forces. Well, not immediately, of course. There were still a few prerequisites I had to complete before formally joining the ranks of the Army. First, I had to graduate from basic training. Then, advanced individual training, or AIT for short. This advanced training is a school tailored specifically to one of the many jobs in the Army. For myself, my job specialty was infantry.

Basic training and AIT for an infantryman take place in one location. In the humid and hot summers of the notorious Ft. Benning Georgia. This is where every soldier in the infantry has stepped foot before becoming a soldier. Unlike other job specialties, such as cooking or mechanics, infantry training was conducted all at once. As a result, basic training and AIT are wrapped into a fourteen-week-long program.

Being an infantryman was pretty straight and to the point. There weren't large books you had to study at night before a test to determine whether you were cut for the job. Instead, the tasks for an infantryman were simplistic in nature. It required determination and physical and mental fortitude, and becoming the master of one thing. Killing. It's as simple of a job description as it gets. Infantrymen were the ones who got down and dirty and met the enemy head-on with pure violence.

While my memory is fuzzy when recalling everything that went on in basic and AIT, a few things stand out. Mostly, how long it all seemed to last. I remember how time seemed to fly by during my stint at Ft. Benning. But, for the most part, it was what you would expect. Drill sergeants yelling at the top of their lungs at new recruits, early wake-up calls to get up and out of bed before the sun rose, and lots of physical training. Early morning exercises, long road marches with weighted packs and weapons.

While at Benning, I made numerous friends who would quickly become my brothers in arms. Forty to fifty guys living in small quarters, long-lasting friendships are bound to occur. Each recruit in basic had their own personal reasons and choices for being there. Some for paid college after enlisting, some for the signing bonuses that came along with joining. However, we chose to be there willingly and knew what we were getting into.

Basic and AIT, for me, wasn't anything that I couldn't handle. I was already in pretty good shape, and there wasn't much the drill sergeants could throw at me that I wasn't physically prepared for. I can thank my coaches throughout my school years playing football for that. Always pushing me to be the best I could be on the field. As for my persistence and never giving up, I owe that trait to my dad. Regardless of the situation, his never give up attitude rubbed off on me at a very young age.

Those fourteen weeks at Benning came and went in a flash. Before I knew it, I was awarded my blue cord, a military decoration worn on the right shoulder of every infantryman, upon graduating from Basic training and AIT. I was officially a member of the United States military. However, I had no idea that my training and all I needed to learn had only begun.

After graduation and a few days' break, I was off to my first duty station. A duty station is where the rubber meets the road in the military. It was where a soldier could train and perform their specific duties. But, unlike basic training, a duty station is where you get to meet those you will be fighting alongside and prepare for our inevitable fate. Going off to war.

My duty station happened to be in

Germany. A much different environment than I was used to. Being in Germany was something I could never have imagined if I hadn't joined the army. The closest I had ever come to leaving the states after fleeing Mexico was through history class textbooks.

I was a young, eighteen-year-old kid when I arrived at my station in Germany. While young, I wasn't the only one in my new unit, fresh out of high school. A few dozen eighteen-year-old, baby-faced young men were there as well. All of them are from various walks of life throughout the United States. All of whom I would have the distinct privilege and honor to fight by their side.

Overall, my new unit's ages varied a wide range. The upper leadership was well into their late thirties and forty's. Those immediately in charge of me, my team, and squad leaders, were in their twenties. Most of them had already seen combat in Iraq or Afghanistan. But, despite the age differences, we shared one thing in common. All of us were there to get our fair share of payback on behalf of the American people.

"Whatever you think you know or learned while you were at basic, you can forget it now. Everything you need to know that will save your life and the lives of others begin here. This is your home now, and every man that wears the same unit patch on their shoulder is your brother." SSG. Campos said, showing me around and introducing me to my squad.

SSG. Campos was my squad leader and had been with the unit for over three years. He was what I considered to be a seasoned, war-hardened soldier. Especially because he's experienced his fair of combat, having been a part of the initial Iraq invasion. When SSG. Campos spoke, I was sure to listen and took everything he said as if his words were made of gold.

Also a South Texas native, Campos stood at five feet, ten inches with a barrel chest. He had a Texas accent that was far from intimidating and had a welcoming tone when talking. Like many of us with Texas roots, being Hispanic, Campos was

Lone Star to his core. Still proud to be Mexican, he wore his proud heritage just as well as his Texas pride. Something that I believe makes Texas such a unique place. However, I knew that SSG. Campos wasn't someone to take lightly or question his kindness for weakness. Along with his welcoming personality, he carried a pair of eyes that looked as if they had witnessed hell on more than one occasion.

I couldn't have asked for a more pleasant and smooth transition into my unit. Everyone was welcoming, from my team leader and squad leader to our battalion commander. It made learning and training under their leadership and training easy to grasp. If I ever had an issue with something or didn't at first understand, I never had an issue finding someone to help me out.

While what I learned differed from what I was taught in basic training, the game's name was unchanged. To become as proficient of a warfighter as possible and be prepared when the call comes to deploy. For those I served with, this call wasn't a matter of if it would happen. But when.

We were almost guaranteed to see combat. The infantry, who arrived at the cutting edge of battle by multiple means of transportation, was in high demand. The war in Iraq seemed far from over, and the Afghanistan occupation was an ongoing battle. However, my unit found great success fighting in the urban environment of Iraq. Multiple presidential citations and silver and bronze stars filled the ranks of my battalion. A battalion that's shown its capabilities in war, there wasn't a reason why we wouldn't deploy.

I remember hearing rumors about a few possible cities we could deploy around the battalion. However, nothing was set in stone. But, based on the reporting from the news, it looked like Baghdad, Iraq's capital, was most likely. I would listen to combat stories circulated in my platoon, playing them out like a movie in my head. In some ways, I was a little jealous of them and what they've done in combat.

I was somewhat envious that most of the

guys in my platoon had real-world experience under their belts. Some of their war stories sounded like something movies are made of. The kind that every soldier wishes they were a part of. And if you weren't there, you couldn't officially be excepted into the warrior fraternity. I wanted to prove to myself and those around me that I was worthy of joining their ranks.

I knew that I was capable of taking on whatever combat could throw at me. Well, that's at least what I had hoped. Of course, no one knows how they'll react when the gunfire and explosions are real. I would like to think that my training paid off, and I could respond necessary when called upon. But it was impossible to say with one hundred percent certainty. I had to experience combat for myself firsthand.

I knew that in the previous year, Iraq was the wild west. Some of the largest battles waged took place during that period, in 2006. Conflicts such as those in Samarra and Baghdad. It was also in this year that Saddam Hussein was executed for his crimes, determined by a trial in court. After his death, a civil war was underway. A power vacuum was created following the execution of Saddam Hussein. Widespread fighting amongst Shias and Sunnis in the region became so violent that the US responded with a build-up of over one hundred and seventy thousand troops.

In the city of Samarra, the leader of the terrorist group Al-Qaeda, Abu Musab al-Zarqawi, was also killed. He Zarqawi led a vicious and bloody campaign against coalition forces in the region before meeting his demise. A US-led air strike, with special operations soldiers on the ground, found his location and dropped hundreds of pounds of ordinance on top of him. After his death, there was a power struggle within the ranks of the terrorist organization. And furthermore, adding to the turmoil troops had to face on the ground.

Unlike Iraq, in 2006, there was a drastic shift in the Afghanistan campaign. Since the invasion in October 2001 and the first half of 2005, major regional offenses had essentially halted. The only major incident in 2006 came after a military vehicle crashed, killing several Afghans. An event that would spark violent, anti-American protests and riots near the city of Kabul. It was the worst since the war began. Although, it was short-lived. The fighting had dwindled significantly, and there wasn't a need to send a large infantry unit to the region.

I didn't know what to expect or if the fighting would be as intense. My only hope was they saved some action for the rest of us, waiting to have our fair share of the war pie.

GAME TIME

A few months had passed since arriving and training with my unit. The training was intense and, at times, stressful. Most of our training focused on urban warfare. Due to my unit's success in Iraq during the invasion of Iraq and the years following, there was a good chance that we would be returning. So, our primary focus was getting brushed up on fighting tactics in the concrete jungle.

I caught on well while training and never let it get the best of me when things got rough. Men like Sgt. Gonzolez and Lambeth, who were my tea leaders, taught me everything I needed to know to stay alive. The younger enlisted guys on my team were there with me nearly every step of the way as well. Guys like Spc. Hartge, Spc. Catterton and Spc. Reyes. All three soldiers in my squad taught me the ropes and everything I needed to know to stay alive. These were the men I would fight next to and put their lives in my hands just as they would have mine.

Since getting to know the guys, it didn't take long to realize what the brotherhood was all about. This brotherhood is what I consider the least talked about topic in the Army. However, it is the most understood. Everyone knows of this sacred relationship. It's the most desired and missed service aspect once returning to civilian life.

Spc. Hartge, Catterton, and Staff Sergent Campos made up only a small portion of the brotherhood I was a part of. Although, they were the guys who I would rely on the most. Hartge was an eighteen-year-old super chill, warm-hearted kid from Indiana who was as tough and strong as nails. You wouldn't be able to judge his superhuman-like strength by size. He stood under five feet seven inches but could outperform guys twice his size. Catterton was one of the first guys I remember conversing with within my squad. We got to know each other's backgrounds and where we came from within a few minutes after meeting. It was as if we were catching up on an old conversation after not seeing each other for years. I viewed him more as my brother than I did as a soldier in arms. Catterton was also a young warfighter, just like myself, waiting to try our hand in combat. A twenty-one-year-old from the midwest who looked like if the army didn't work out, he would have a good career as a Hollister clothing model. He was also a seasoned fighter, having completed a year-long Iraq rotation.

The four of us each shared one dream and, for the most part, had the same views and outlook on life. We wanted to make the enemy pay. Create a world for them, where they were either destroyed or submitted. We wanted to put what we learned and knew on display and test on the battlefield and put our skills to the test.

Despite some of the guys having a few deployments under their belts, they wanted more. They knew the fight wasn't over, and work was to be done. The mission was never complete as long as the enemy had breathed their bodies. Luckily, our dreams would come true sooner than we had expected.

Shit. This is actually happening. I thought to myself. The low pitch humming from the plane's engine, thirty thousand feet in the air, was calming and peaceful. Most of the guys in my platoon slept under the cabins' dim lights, while others managed to read a book or listen to their headphones. I guess that wasn't what I envisioned heading to combat for the first time.

My battalion orders came down from the chain of command, informing us that we were heading to Iraq. Near the small town of Adhamiyah in particular. The area became a stronghold since the invasion, having been unoccupied by troops over the years. Situated in northeast Baghdad along the Tigris River, Adhamiyah was the place to go if you wanted to see action. My battalion was tasked to gain a foothold in the city by eliminating the local enemy militia that polluted the area.

My mind raced sitting on that plane, heading to a wartorn country. Getting any sleep felt nearly impossible on the hours'-long journey. Sure, I was excited to finally be able to contribute and put my skills on display. Hell, it's what I've talked about accomplishing for years now. However, I began overthinking too much and made things more complicated than I'm sure they had to be.

I thought of my family back home and everyone I left behind. It was hard not thinking about them. I hadn't seen them in a couple of years. Only managing to call my mom and dad every once in a while. I reminisced on my childhood growing up under their roof and how far we've all come. My parents meant the world to me, and I wanted nothing more than to make them proud.

I thought about countless potentials and what-if situations that could happen in combat.

And what it would mean to my family if something were to happen to me or I didn't make it back. For example, what would my parents do if they received a call informing them that I would be coming home in a casket? How they would react or what they would think of me.

While trying my hardest not to think about dying, the idea took over my mind. No matter how hard I attempted to brush it off. However, I knew the hazards and the recipe for it to happen were all there. As an infantryman, I quickly realized two facts regarding the nature of our work. You either come home alive, or you don't. It was as simple as that. They were the only things that stayed constant in war.

I remember praying to myself, asking God to take care of my family if he decided to call me home. I asked that he would take the pain from my mother and for my dad to continue to be her rock. If anything were to happen, I didn't want to suffer and wanted it to be a quick death. And if it were to be in a firefight, I asked God to allow me to fight hard and not be scared. I wanted Him to give me the strength I needed to fight to the very end and protect those around me.

I'm unsure if anyone else on the flight shared the same thoughts or concerns as I did. Or if what I was thinking was natural at all. Everything was new to me, and I didn't know what combat would be like. Nevertheless, I had to feel comfortable with what I learned and retained during training. I had to suppress my negative thinking and put them in an emotional box for the time being. Maintaining one hundred percent of my focus on what lay ahead had to be the only thing on my mind. Any other thought would only serve as a hindrance.

"Welcome to your new home, gents!" The battalion commander shouted from the center aisle near the front of the plane.

We landed in a surprisingly quiet environment at the Baghdad international airport late at night. Much different than what I was expecting. Rubbing the crust out of my eyes from the few minutes of sleep I managed to get, I had my first view of Iraq. I stood looking out into the area surrounding the airfield from the tarmac. Having seen countless photos ad video footage of the war-torn country since joining the Army, it wasn't what I had imagined.

A flat, sand and dust-covered terrain that stretched out into the distance as far as I could see. Other than a few tall structures that stood out on the horizon near the city, there wasn't anything that jumped out and grabbed my attention. However, the lack of stable electricity in the region did stand out. While home lighting flickered in and faded out, only a handful of homes had power. However, most were covered in deep, black darkness under the Iraqi night sky.

We were transported from the airfield to our base, where we'd live the next year. Less than a twenty-minute drive on small stick shift buses. The chosen vehicle of choice for moving troops within the green zone. A zone deemed as safe as it was controlled by the US and coalition forces.

Once arriving at our base, I was immediately stunned by the appearance of our living conditions. Honestly, it was nothing like I expected. It was a rundown building that had seen its share of war. Previously hit by mortar fire during the invasion, from its appearance, it looked as if it could have collapsed in on us at any moment. I almost felt sorry for the poor bastards that occupied it when it blew up.

After the invasion, US troops took control of most of the infrastructure that wasn't destroyed by bombs. A far cry from one of Saddam Hussein's gold and marble palaces, our living conditions beat sleeping in the dirt under the hot sun. Besides, we didn't sign up and volunteer with the expectation of staying at a Holiday Inn. We were there to fight a war. But, if the living conditions were somehow better than expected, it was a welcomed amenity.

I adjusted to the deployment lifestyle faster than I expected. I had a timeframe set for how long it would take me to get used to things before deploying. Although, I somehow beat my expectations and faced my life in Iraq quite easily. I guess I can contribute most of that to the pace of the deployment thus far. We hit the ground running at a sprinter's speed, leaving no room to worry about anything other than staying alive.

While I still thought about what could happen and the occasional onset of fear, there wasn't any spare time to allow it to consume me. Within the first few weeks of arriving in country, I had a few dozen missions and several firefights credited to my name. Thus far, Adhamiyah was living up to its name, throwing everything it could at us. I had encountered almost daily: sniper fire, ambushes, mortar and rocket attacks, and IEDs.

However, out of the recipe of everything that could kill us, IEDs were what I feared the most. Like most of the dialog in the military, the term IED is a military acronym. It stands for an improvised explosive device. Essentially, these devices are homemade bombs employed by the enemy to attack US and coalition forces.

IEDs were typically crude in their

construction. They could be made of nearly anything Al-Qaeda could get their hands on. Unexploded ordinance, such as an old artillery shell, or an empty box, could be used to make an IED. I've even seen the enemy go as far as using the gutted carcass of a dead animal. That was the mindset of who we were facing. Anything was fair game in their eyes. They would do whatever they had to, as long as it had the potential to kill Americans and our allies.

Unlike gunfire, IEDs were hard to defend against. At least when I was getting shot at, I could shoot back. Even under a mortar attack, I had the option of running, taking cover, or hearing them rain down from above. IEDs were a special breed of weapon in a category of their own. Metal detectors were unhelpful if the device was made of something other than metal. They were nearly invisible to even the seasoned infantryman. If you somehow managed to spot one, however, chances were that it was too late.

What I hated most about these explosive

devices were the various ways they could be detonated. The earlier models, during the invasion, were rudimentary in how they worked. For example, they could be triggered using a trip wire or pull string once their target was in the blast radius. Much different now, however, as they've advanced technologically. They can be detonated with a cell phone, miles away, or by the pressure caused when stepping or driving over one.

Working in a congested environment like Adhamiyah, my unit found that getting from point A to point B was best accomplished on a set of wheels. Relying solely on the boots on our feet, with no means of a fast extraction, wasn't the best option in our playbook. A prolonged firefight in the city, pinned down, would be a disaster with countless dead or wounded. In addition, the helicopters found difficulty finding a place to land in our area of operation. Or they were busy providing airlift services for the special operation guys.

Humvees, a four-wheeled, light-armored

versatile vehicle, was our preferred means of transportation. As an infantryman riding through a city like Adhamiyah, IEDs made my job a nightmare. The trash that littered the Iraqi streets meant they could be hidden anywhere. An explosive device could be placed in one of the numerous potholes that filled the streets.

While I had encountered a few IEDs, they were on a smaller scale in terms of the damage they could produce. However, they seemed to be packing more punch than the one that blew up before. Luckily, the IEDs I was unfortunate enough to experience only caused minor bumps, scrapes, and bruises. For the guys in my squad and with whom I shared a vehicle, surviving an explosion was like a right of passage.

As one of the new guys on the team, I was given the task of being a machine gunner. While in the Humvee, my job was to operate a .50 caliber machine gun mounted on the top. Standing through the center hatch, a hole in the center of the vehicle's roof, gave me a three hundred and sixty-degree view of the battlefield. If there were a threat that presented itself, I had the best vantage point to see and engage it.

Being the gunner on top of the Humvee was also where I felt I learned the art of war the fastest as a new guy. You were forced to adapt to the environment if you wanted to survive and keep your team safe. All your senses are sent into overdrive, standing exposed outside the gunner's hatch, unlike the rest of the squad, tucked inside the vehicle's armored interior. As a result, I had an unobstructed overhead view of the battlefield.

Watching the teams work on the ground was like reading a football playbook. Each soldier has their own specified job and task they had to perform. If executed correctly, as it usually went without a hitch, I was fortunate to witness the chaotic symphony of war. Controlled violence that's taken us months and years to master.

It felt good to get my feet wet in this hellish country. It was hard not to think and realize what we'd already accomplished. We've survived multiple firefights and touched death on more than one occasion. All the while facing the enemy head-on and never backing down from a fight. As long as my brothers were standing next to me, I felt invisible. Like I could accomplish anything. And the only thing there was to fear was failing them.

However, it felt like I had the world's weight on my shoulders every now and then. After one particular mission, I remember when the realization of war finally hit me. It was the first time I took a moment to acknowledge the gravity of what I was witnessing and experiencing.

My platoon returned from a patrol in the heart of Adhamiyah at night and returned to base. Most of us try to calm our nerves from the adrenaline high earlier. While on patrol, our Humvees were caught in an ambush while on a movement to contact (MTC) operation. An operation that was routine for us, and we knew what to expect. An MTC was what it implies. Our platoon would move through the city until we made contact with the enemy.

Thankfully none of us were injured during the firefight that night. Although, there were enough close calls to raise the hairs on the back of my neck. Bullets buzzed and popped by my head as I handled the .50 cal machine gun.

After returning to base and sitting on a bench near a fire pit, I decided to have a cigarette. A smoke break became somewhat of a ritual after a mission. While it wasn't the healthiest decision, it was one of the only occasions I had time to decompress. Even if it were just a few minutes. Then, a thought dawned on me as my break neared its end. Out of nowhere, it hit me like a ten-ton brick.

Here I was, facing the hazards of a warzone, and I hadn't seen my twenty-first birthday. I couldn't legally buy an alcoholic drink nor rent a car. And yet, here I am, a soldier deployed to Iraq, fighting for my country. And not that it mattered, because it came along with the job; I was responsible for taking the life of a few human beings. Since being deployed, it was the only time that the surrealness of where I was and what I was doing set in.

After years of waiting and training, I was finally here. Doing what I felt was best in defense of my country. All before enjoying a nice, ice, cold, foam-topped beer.

CONTACT

BOOM!

"IED!" I shouted without hesitation. By now, I didn't have to look where the sound originated behind me to know what it was.

"That's our alarm clock!" SSG. Campos yelled up at me, tugging on my leg from inside our Humvee.

"That's one hell of an alarm clock, Staff Sergent!" I shouted back at him, grinning down from my gunner's hatch.

We were on patrol in Adhamiyah in a five-vehicle convoy, and each carried five soldiers from the platoon. My vehicle was positioned third within the formation. The last Humvee in our convoy triggered an IED, setting it off as it drove over. Luckily, it didn't do much damage or injure anyone. The explosion only managed to knock off one of the spare tires secured on the vehicle's rear.

SSG. Campos was right. It was time to get back on my A-game, out of the sleepy fog I was in. I was working on less than six hours of sleep in two days. Our operation tempo was in overdrive. We were conducting missions throughout the city daily. Sometimes, running two patrols a day in search of Al-Qaeda. Days when we managed to find time to ourselves, we spent it in our beds, trying to get some shut-eye.

We departed our base and into the city early that morning, before sunrise that day, May 14, 2007. The hands of the clocks in our ready room were approaching six o'clock local time. The patrol started off like any other. A routine patrol through the streets of Adhamiyah, searching for enemy activity.

Other than the IED exploding, we hadn't seen any signs of the enemy. There wasn't anything that stood out or raised any alarm that this patrol would be any different. Instead, I found it difficult to keep my eyes from closing due to boredom. I was used to the activity and action the city typically provided. Perhaps to the point where I took the lack thereof for granted.

The nature of combat was an environment that I had adapted to. Iraq has been my home for the past eleven months, closing in on one year in war. There wasn't much that Adhamiyah could throw at me that I hadn't seen before. I knew what to expect here and became callused about my surroundings. Reacting to enemy fire or an IED was like breathing to me. However, I feared that I was becoming too comfortable. Perhaps too complacent.

This is why guys in special operations units had significantly shorter deployments. While ours were measured in years, theirs were in months. Due to their high operation tempo and missions, they tended to burn out fast. A vital contributor to the war, special operations deployments were reduced in time to keep them fresh.

According to studies of troops deployed, complacency is one of the effects of prolonged combat. This phenomenon is better known to soldiers as "Ground Hog Day Syndrome." A term based on the popular movie where the main character is forced to relive the same day. Over and over again. A soldier begins to feel overconfident in his abilities and feels they could do it in their sleep. When the fact is, they can not.

Complacency is as deadly as bullets whizzing by our heads or buried IEDs. Nonetheless, shorter deployments were a luxury we didn't have. No matter the operation tempo or how tired we were.

"Contact! Three o'clock, one hundred meters. Small arms fire coming from the building over there!" I shouted at the top of my lungs for everyone in my Humvee to hear.

About an hour after the IED explosion struck the rear vehicle, enemy fire erupted from our right side. AK-47 and machine-gun fire focused on the two Humvees in front of me. Chips of pavement from the street kicked up as bullets skipped off the ground near them. I could also see the sparks erupting from the side of the Humvee from being hit with accurate gunfire. If it were not for the armor, everyone inside would have been shredded.

Usually, in a situation like this, the first vehicles would normally turn and face the enemy to engage. However, they could not maneuver and get themselves into position. Parked cars along the side of the road prevented them from doing so. With enemy fire continuing to actively engage our convoy, we had to react quickly. Otherwise, we'd be sitting ducks and allowing the enemy to gain the upper hand.

Making a tactical decision, with limited space to move, the first two vehicles in the convoy decided to push forward. Continuing to drive rather than turning. Doing so would allow them to get out of the kill zone and my Humvee to engage from a better position. A side street nearest to my vehicle and adjacent to the incoming fire. Unfortunately, it would take a few seconds to get into place and away from the main convoy, but it was our best shot.

We knew the streets of Adhamiyah well. Nearly as well, if not more, than we knew the roads back in the states. We had to be because our lives depended on our knowledge of them. There weren't too many places the enemy could hide and prevent us from being able to engage them. Regardless of where the enemy attacked, a road was always nearby that led to them.

My heart began racing and pounded inside my chest as we made our way down a narrow side street. The blood coursing through my veins felt as if it were boiling inside. And the dose of adrenaline I was experiencing was unlike any other I had before. While I was pissed that the enemy decided to attack us, I welcomed the fight. It was the only thing that managed to work and get me out of the mental fog I was in.

"Contact!" I shouted.

I saw sparks and small puffs of smoke emitting inside and around a building less than one hundred meters from us. Everything around me seemed to be happening at half speed as we rolled closer. I had a white knuckle grasp firmly gripping the handle on my mounted .50 cal before swinging and pointing it toward the enemy. While this was the first time I killed someone, the experience was always the same. It was an act I didn't shy away from or was hesitant to perform. Although, it wasn't something I wanted to get used to.

I began returning fire, pressing down on the butterfly-style trigger of my weapon. Letting out long and sustained bursts of fire. Projectiles over two inches in length, designed to produce as much destruction as possible on the enemy. The .50 cal was capable of penetrating armor and concrete barriers. But, when it comes in contact with flesh, it evaporates it. Turning a body into a burst of bright red and pink colored water vapor.

I aimed at the enemy, not choosing one in particular. The .50 cal wasn't a point-and-shoot precision rifle. Instead, this was an area weapon. A weapon is designed to engage targets over a large area, not an individual target, one at a time.

Moments later, I saw the tale sign that one of my rounds hit its mark. A man who I was looking at, shooting from behind a concrete slab in the street, vanished. His body vaporized, leaving behind his shredded pieces of clothing falling to the ground. Then seconds later, another body. Exploding into a misty, pink cloud.

After engaging and killing two from the group shooting at us, the remaining two Humvees were pulling in behind me. Seeing them roll in behind us is a feeling I'll never forget. It was like a scene cut out from a movie. Two armored Humvees come in as death, and the unknown surrounds them before they begin returning fire. Knowing I had these guys out here to have my back felt good.

With three vehicles now returning the hate, the enemy fire subsided. Not completely, but enough for us to push forward and meet up with the first two squads. My Humvee was the first in order and took the lead. We went down the narrow street for a couple hundred meters before making a few turns connecting us to our original route. As we pushed forward, the vehicle behind us would provide cover. Then, the second Humvee would do the same, with the third watching out for them.

My senses were in hyperdrive. I focused all my attention on where the enemy fled and where they could potentially be. In training, we referred to this as observing the likely, known, and suspected. Doing so gave the enemy less chance to catch us off-guard and ambush us again.

That's odd...I remember thinking to myself. Knowing these roads as well as I did, I knew something was out of place. I knew something wasn't right. Although, I couldn't place a finger on what it was.

Our Humvee rolled over what felt like a

large speed bump in the middle of the road. However, I knew this to be impossible. For as long as I've driven these streets, there hasn't been a speed bump here before. In fact, the only speed bumps that I've encountered were on base and never on the Iraqi streets. So I wondered if anyone else in our vehicle noticed or if we hit something I didn't see.

Suddenly, in a blinding light and deafening sound, there wasn't a need to question anymore. What we ran over was far from being something as innocent as a speed bump, rock, or misplaced item left in the street. Instead, it was an IED. One that was unlike the others I've come in contact with in Iraq. This IED, I knew, had to be much larger and packed one hell of a punch.

Disoriented and confused, I still managed to comprehend a few things. The first was that I was airborne. I knew that my body was suspended in the air after the explosion. I couldn't tell if I were still in the vehicle or had flown out through the hatch. Second, I was sure I would more than likely be injured. To what extent, I had no clue.

I wouldn't find out until later that we were blown over five feet into the air from an IED weighing more than two hundred pounds. Significantly larger than anything we've come close to encountering. The average size of an IED was twenty-five to fifty pounds, about the size of a briefcase. On the other hand, a two hundred pound IED was equivalent to ten propane tanks packed with explosives. Enough to disable an M1 Abram tank. The Humvees we traveled in served little in protecting against a blast as large as this one.

IEDs in 2007 was a huge problem for coalition forces in Iraq. During this time, sixty-three percent of coalition deaths were caused by IEDs. Moreover, they were such an issue that the odds of hitting an IED were greater than avoiding them altogether. So for us on the ground, it was only a matter of time before we had to pay the price.

Then, in what seemed like it had taken forever, our vehicle slammed back onto the ground below in a thunderous crash.

"Shit!" I screamed as loud as possible, along with a few options of chosen expletives.

What I was experiencing remains complicated to comprehend or put into words. But, it was the most pain I had ever felt. Excruciating, mind-numbing, burning pain surged through my body, from the bottom of my feet to the top of my head. Everything hurt.

The force of the impact caused both of my legs to give out from under me. My legs crumbled like a cardboard box under my weight, dumping me into the vehicle's interior. My head slammed into the lap of one of my squad members. I couldn't hear much of anything around me or if anyone was shooting. An ear-piercing ring rang from inside my brain, making exterior noises sound muffled and difficult to distinguish.

As I lay there, I looked to see whose body I had fallen on and if they were okay. It was Spc. Hartge. After my focus, still a bit hazy, came in contact with his eyes, I immediately knew his fate. He was dead. A blank, void glaze washed over his eyes. I didn't need a medic to confirm what I saw or felt as I looked up at him. The lively spark that filled my brother's gaze was gone.

As much as I felt like crying and shouting out in grief, I couldn't. My emotions seemed too much to bear, and my body struggled to express them. I was tired of seeing my brothers lose their lives in combat. I felt that our unit had seen and had its fair share of death during this deployment. Before this patrol, my unit suffered the loss of fourteen soldiers. They were brothers, fathers, and sons. It was an honor to have served next to them.

Sgt. Flemming and Spc. Catterton, also in my vehicle, jumped out and into the street. Both of them were on fire. They were moving as fast as they could to escape and somehow smother the fire. However, from my traumatized perspective, it looked as if they were moving slowly, at one-fourth the speed they could, and momentarily pausing in time. Unfortunately, their efforts failed as the fire grew and began engulfing their bodies. They continued to run around outside the vehicle a few feet from me. I could feel anger rising inside me, unable to help them. All that I could do at the moment was observe their firey bodies.

Laying in the lap of Spc. Hartge, it was the closest that I'd come to giving up. Death and destruction surrounded me, and I was in too much pain to do anything about it. I knew that the IED had taken one life; at that moment, I felt I was witnessing two more. Serving with these guys, bound together by a bond forged in fire, it was like a piece of me died along with them.

Our Humvee was on fire, and I had difficulty getting my bodily functions to work. And as I lay there, I made my peace with God. A God that I neglected and resented throughout this deployment. As the number of casualties increased, my faith took a turn in the opposite direction. I was pissed at God. I questioned why He would allow these good soldiers to be taken so soon.

I tried to reconnect to the God I grew up trusting and the one, my mom, prayed to daily. The same God I know led us safely across the Mexico border and into the United States. I wanted him to hear me again and prayed that he hadn't forgotten my voice. I knew this would be my last moment, and I wanted my soul to be where I needed it to be.

While in prayer, I asked God for forgiveness for my lack of faith. I prayed that he would look over my mom and hope she would somehow find peace, knowing I was gone. I wanted my younger brother to be strong and that he would know what to do, taking my spot as the oldest sibling. I asked God that my sister would find happiness in everything she does and will do in the future. Finally, I asked my Father in Heaven to let my dad know that I served my country with honor and pride, and I hope I made them all proud.

War is known to cause an individual to question their faith or religion. It had the capability of taking the fabric of what you believe in and ripping it out of you. Growing up, believing that a higher power of love and kindness exists can fade away like paper in the wind. The events that occur in combat are hellish. They consist of only the things believed to exist in horror films and nightmares. When someone has a first-hand account of these horrors, it changes and affects them. War can change and alter who you are and what you are, right down to the depths of your soul.

I couldn't envision that I could somehow be severely wounded and somehow manage to live a normal life. As I've mentioned, the reality of an infantryman, you either came home alive or under an American flag-draped box. These were the two constant factors that came with the nature of war. These two facts were as solid as the earth beneath your feet. There were no in-betweens, ins, or outs. They were the rules of war, and the two came with the territory.

After praying, I closed my eyes and prepared to meet my creator. Although I wasn't necessarily ready to die, I still considered myself a young kid. If I wasn't in my current situation, I knew I would know many life and accomplishments ahead of me.

"Get out, man!" I heard a voice, grumbling in pain, shout aloud.

I slowly opened my eyes and looked at where the voice came from. It was Campos. He grabbed my leg and shook it violently, thinking that I was unconscious or worse. Looking at him, I could see that he was stuck in the passenger seat.

Campos's equipment melted to his seat, preventing him from getting out. It looked like his gear was thrown in an oven and then placed on his body. The intense fire in and around our vehicle felt like we were parked on the sun's surface.

"No, bro. I'm done. This is for me." In my current state of mind, I responded, shouting back at him with all the strength I could muster.

Given my situation and the pain I was in, I knew that my time had come. I had already made peace with God and was ready to depart my body. There was nothing that could have convinced me otherwise.

Despite wanting to give up, a small part of me was stunned to hear and talk with Campos.

Thinking that I was the sole, last standing survivor of my Humvee, I was shocked to listen to his voice. Initially, I couldn't see anyone else in the vehicle with me after Flemming and Catterton managed to get out alive, despite being engulfed in flames. And, I knew that Hartge was dead.

I was equally comforted conversing with Campos. Even as brief as our conversation lasted, I was glad I wouldn't be alone if I was going to die. I guess he was silent due to a loss of consciousness. But I wasn't sure. He may have been in the same boat as me, thinking he was alone and dying. And the only reason he spoke up was from the sounds of my crying in the seat behind him.

No! Not today. This will not be where you die! An inner voice jolted me back to reality and the mindset that I was in. Despite having no audible sound, the voice within me was fierce and shook me from inside.

The voice was one of reason, determination, and full of fight. It wasn't something that I was telling myself or what I was thinking at the time.

Instead, this voice was like an inner beam of light that ignited from within my soul. Out of the experiences I've had in combat, this was the first time that I ever had a spiritual encounter such as this.

Gathering the last bit of strength that I had in me, I sat my body upright and pulled myself back into the gunners' hatch. Everything I touched was like touching a stovetop that's been left on high for hours. Finding a bearable spot that wasn't blazing hot was impossible. The entire Humvee was smoldering and on fire.

Finally, after getting my body through the hatch, I got back on my .50 cal machine gun. Despite wanting to die a few moments ago, I knew Campos relied on me. I could have cared less for myself and accepted my fate if he were not with me. I couldn't have gone on, knowing Campos would survive, if only I used my last breath fighting to the end.

I knew that if there was any chance of Campos getting out alive, I needed to provide covering fire. Putting some lead down range at the enemy would allow the guys in the Humvees behind us to pull him out to safety. I remember learning in training that the best medicine on the battlefield is firepower. And, there was no better way to administer this medicine than with an M2 .50 cal. First, killing the enemy before treating the wounded.

Standing there in the gunners' hatch was also the first time I could assess the extent of the damage. My eyesight was still hazy as smoke and flames rose around me. From my topside view, the Humvee looked like it had been through a meat grinder. It was almost unrecognizable at first. Two hundred pounds of explosives detonating beneath us turned our armored two-ton vehicle into a tin can.

I grabbed the handles of the machine gun and oriented to the last location I saw the enemy fighters.

"Fuck you!" I shouted in anger, hoping my vulgar words would somehow assist in destroying the enemy.

One armor-piercing projectile exited the barrel of my rifle and impacted the building I was shooting at before. Keeping pressure on the trigger, I expected a second, third, fourth, and fifth to follow the same path. However, this wasn't what took place. After firing the first round, the second created an explosion in the gun's barrel.

The intense heat from the fire, coupled with the explosion that occurs when a gun is fired, was a destructive mix. The second bullet never left the gun. Thus, rendering the weapon inoperable. There wasn't a quick solution or remedy to fix the problem. It was nothing more than a large, hot metal paperweight.

Without having the security the .50 cal provided, I fell back into a state of despair. If I couldn't kill the enemy, I believed we didn't stand a chance of surviving.

Boom! A second explosion rumbled from beneath me.

Unlike the blast from the IED, this one was

significantly smaller. I initially thought there were multiple IEDs, and the enemy set them off one by one. A tactic known to coalition soldiers as the Daisy chain during the war. Enemy fighters would string together multiple IEDs along the road. Detonating the first one would result in the destruction or disabling of a targeted vehicle. The remaining IEDs would then be triggered upon assisting forces arriving on the scene or as the wounded fled onto the street.

The second explosion pushed me back against the hatch, rattling the bones inside my body. Finally, after gaining my orientation, I realized what the blast was. It came from inside the vehicle, behind me, and close to my feet. Looking in that direction, I knew that's where we stored a few of the grenades we carried while on patrol.

The fire that raged beneath, on the floor of our Humvee, caused one of the grenades to explode. A condition that is known as cooking off. To my disbelief, Campos nor myself were injured in the blast. I concluded that the big man upstairs still had a plan for me, preventing the grenade's shrapnel from causing us further harm.

With no other immediate options, I decided it was best to exit. From outside the vehicle, I knew there was a chance. Even if my odds were slim, I believed I could pull Campos from the wreckage and to safety. So, from the hatch, I grabbed my small sidearm. A pistol I stored next to me and began climbing up and onto the roof of the Humvee. My first thought was that I would be able to leap onto the engine. It was the sturdiest part amidst the twisted metal and nearest to Campos. Then, I would try to pull him through the windshield frame and onto the street.

However, my planned course of action was immediately halted. A large, raging fire that rose feet into the air from the engine prevented me from doing so. If there were any chance of survival, jumping into an inferno wasn't in my best interest. I was in enough pain as it was. I knew I had little chance of surviving the flames, and the pain was something I wasn't ready to face.

Running low on options, I had to make a split-second decision. The only thing that wasn't on fire immediately around me was the paved street below. While I knew the distance to the ground was something I could survive, it appeared like a cliff's ledge from my position. And, when I jumped, it would have taken seconds to reach the bottom.

Here goes nothin'. I mumbled under my voice.

Before committing to the jump, I said a silent prayer. I knew there would be some pain. But, to what extent, I wasn't sure. Then, as my feet and body hit the ground, sharp pain pulsated and burned throughout both of my legs. I knew something was terribly wrong. The pain was so intense that it made it nearly impossible to stand. Unknown to me, my legs suffered massive damage during the IED blast from compound fractures in both femurs.

After the jump, the pain in my legs was enough to cause me to scream out loud. A pain that made me feel as if I could have stayed there, on the ground, and died. And, there was a strange sensation of bitter metal taste of copper I had in the back of my throat. Like a handful of pennies, I decided to stick a handful of them in my mouth and chew them. Although, what I tasted was far from metal or copper. It was my own blood that was spilling down my esophagus from my face and nose.

While unable to stand, it wasn't my only concern. For the first time, I saw the full extent of my injuries. I recognized that some of the flames I saw around me in the Humvee were coming from my body. My uniform and equipment were engulfed in fire and smoke, burning into my flesh.

The smell of my skin burning and the sound of it popping is something I will live with forever. Whatever hopes I had of saving Campos dwindled once again. By now, I knew that death must have been my only destiny.

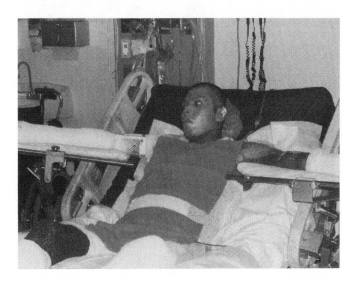

STOP, DROP, AND ROLL

Stop, drop, and roll. That's what they used to tell us in grade school if we ever found ourselves on fire. I remember our teachers making the kids practice the drill in the nineties during class. But, of course, I'm sure none of us imagined that any of us would be in a situation as such. So, we rarely took the drill seriously, and it was usually an excuse to play around on the floor.

Now, as I lay in the street of Adhamiyah on fire, I was almost thankful for the childhood training. However, that was until I began the three-step process of extinguishing the fire that covered most of my body. I'm sure I must have been a confusing sight for the onlookers in the city as I rolled and flopped on the ground. I closed my eyes and moved my body from one side to the other as fast as possible. The fire closest to the ground and under my body briefly went out as I smothered it. Then, as I rolled over to my other side, the fire would ignite again as if nothing had happened. It was a pattern that repeated itself, regardless of what I did or how fast I rolled.

This shit doesn't work. Who even thought of this? Was the guy who thought this up ever on fire to know it worked? Whoever that guy is, I hope he knows that his method sucks major ass. I remember thinking to myself. And at the same time, continuing to repeat the process for as long as I could physically take it.

During that moment, it was the only time I was able to make fun of my situation. I'm not sure if it was my mind's response to the pain I was in. Or, it was because that was the person I was known to be at times. After I get out of my head and want to give up, all there is left to do is make the best I can out of a terrible situation. I seriously questioned the validity of the stop, drop, and roll procedure and if it worked. Perhaps it may have, had it not been for my fuel-dowsed clothing.

Then, as I was about to give something a try to diminish my flaming body, a large, white cloud began covering me. The cloud was so thick that it prevented me from getting a breath of air and clogged my airway. It was coming from a fellow warfighter in one of the parked Humvees. He managed to get his hands on a fire extinguisher and ran over to put the fire out. It took him a few seconds, but his efforts were a success.

"I'm going to try and find us some help, brother. Don't go anywhere. I'll be right back!" He said, standing over me. My skin continued smoking and burning from the fire.

"No shit! Look at me." I sarcastically responded before he ran back towards his Humvee, parked less than fifty yards from me.

As my brother-in-arms ran for help, I saw that the guys in the two Humvees were actively engaging the enemy. A sporadic yet, concentrated fire continued around us. Laying on the ground, I could hear loud cracks overhead from incoming small arms fire. Unfortunately, I couldn't determine where the shooting was coming from. My best guess was that the enemy fire appeared to be coming from all around us from three locations. We were surrounded.

Some time had passed since having been extinguished. I initially thought that maybe I was forgotten. My guys fighting the enemy took precedence over me, which was something I completely understood. I'd rather them kill as many of those fuckers as they could rather than come back for me. And by its looks, I was sure Campos didn't survive. The fire in my vehicle continued to burn, sending a pillar of black smoke into the air.

Moments later, using as much cover as I could from incoming rounds, I heard the distant sound of a helicopter in the distance. Then, looking above me, two Blackhawk helicopters flew directly above my position. They began circling our location at a high-speed rate, which seemed to be a few feet above the rooftops. I initially assumed they were there to pick me up and extract me. Perhaps I wasn't left behind, and my guys called a medivac to get the wounded and dead out of the area. Unfortunately, this wasn't the case.

Instead, the Blackhawks were conducting an operation nearby in the vicinity of where we were located. The smoke rising from my Humvee acted as a beacon of distress, and the pilots figured they would check it out. Circling above, the pilots had a birdseye view of nearly the entire city. According to the reports, I would read later, the pilots contacted our commander and informed him of our dire situation.

From the pilot's perspective, they estimated anywhere from thirty to thirty-five enemy fighters closing in on our position. Carrying everything from RPKs, and rocket-propelled grenade launchers, to pistols and AK-47s. The two-hundred-pound IED we ran over stirred a hornet's nest of fighters out looking for blood. They were coming in from multiple avenues and angles. All of them, I'm sure, hoped that they would collect the bodies of our dead and finish off whoever stood in their way. If it weren't for the brave pilots and crew of the Blackhawks, the enemy's wishes might have very well come true.

Suddenly, from above me, I heard what appeared to be someone starting up a weedwhacker. Then, a few seconds later, the sounds of metallic pings and clinks all around me.

Hell yes! Light em' up! I said out loud, only after realizing what the noises were.

The Blackhawk helicopters began shooting at the enemy closing in on us. As they circled overhead for another pass, their empty shell casings from fired rounds fell to the ground. What I thought to be the sounds of a weedwhacker were the Blackhawks .50 cal and 7.62mm machine guns firing simultaneously. It was a welcoming sound to hear and gave me the extra strength to stay in the fight. Who knows what our fate would have been if it weren't for the pair of Blackhawks saving our asses?

The pilots had it in their minds that they wouldn't leave until every threat was eliminated. So pass after pass overhead, the pair of helicopters were actively engaged in the fight. I knew whoever they were shooting at was no match against their superior firepower.

After the Blackhawks' firing finally ceased, more than thirty enemy fighters lay dead in the Iraqi streets when it was all said and done. They made one last pass over me and returned to the airfield to restock and resupply. It felt good to breathe again, without the sounds of enemy bullets aimed to kill me. While my body was still in great pain, not being actively targeted by guys wanting to shoot me provided temporary relief.

"Hey! You alive?" A soldier stopped as he ran past me and leaned in to ask. I wasn't sure if I decided to doze off and nap on purpose, but I must have. The little strength I had left was completely drained and forced me to rest, regardless of whether I wanted to.

The clothes on my body, covered in

chemicals from the fire extinguisher, continued to smoke and make strange noises as they cooled off. It appeared like I had smoke seeping from every nook and cranny of my body. I'm sure if I were in someone else's shoes, I would have assumed I were dead too.

At first, the soldier's face was hard to make out, but after a few seconds, I saw that it was SSG. Nuñes. He was one of the squad leaders parked in the second Humvee behind me. He was an average-sized muscular soldier with a stern, chiseled jawline who knew his way around a warzone.

"I'm alive. Well, I think I am." I responded after taking a moment to catch my breath. After all that I had been through, I hoped I was alive, and this wasn't the afterlife. If so, this wasn't the place I intended on staying for eternity.

"Can you walk?" He asked.

"I think my legs are broken, I can't tell, but they hurt like hell, sergeant."

SSG. Nuñes took a slight step back and glanced over my legs.

"You're good to go. Let's move." He said assuringly. Hell, he could have told me that I was submerged in ice water, and I probably would have believed him. I trusted SSG. Nuñes's with my life and thought highly of him. So if he says my legs are fine, they had to be.

"Roger that, sergeant. Can you help me up?" I asked.

As he helped me to my feet, we began walking toward his Humvee. I hobbled and skipped as best as I could while supporting my weight on his shoulder. My legs were still in pain, making the short distance feel like we had traveled for miles.

"I'll have to let you stand on your own for a second while I open the door. Can you manage to do that for me, soldier?" SSG. Nuñes asked after arriving at his vehicle.

"Roger, sergeant. I think I'll be fine."

As SSG. Nuñes released his grip from my side and turned to open the passenger door; I collapsed. My legs buckled from beneath me, unable to support my weight and causing me to tumble over.

"Are you okay?" Nuñes asked me, with genuine concern expressed over his stern facial features.

"I'm all good, brother," I responded, chuckling as I grimaced in pain.

"You crazy SOB." He laughed. "Are you in any pain?"

"Negative! I'm good to go."

I was on such an adrenaline high that I had forgotten how much pain I was in. Reuniting with my brothers after all this chaos numbed the pain coursing throughout my body. SSG. Nuñes helped me back on my feet and finally got me inside the vehicle. The inside of a Humvee that wasn't on fire and full of blood was a sight for sore eyes. It felt like I was stepping into a five-star hotel after being on the road for months. The seats felt as soft as marshmallows, and the interior was cool to my skin. Even though there wasn't any air conditioning.

As soon as I was seated, one of our platoon medics ran over and began treating me. Ripping off most of my clothing and bandaged up my bloody and open wounds. As the medic worked, aggressively trying to stop the bleeding, all I could think of was how thankful I was to have made it out. Whatever pain I felt was nothing compared to my guys who didn't make it and shared the same fate as me.

The driver, seated in front of me, was shocked by my sight. I guess I couldn't have blamed him. He was fairly new to the platoon, having flown in midway through our deployment. I've only seen him occasionally in passing on base, and he mostly kept to himself. This was the first time he left the wire and faced the enemy in combat. I would be shocked, too, if today's patrol was the first combat experience I witnessed. In a drastic turn of events, what started as an anticlimactic boring patrol, became a literal hell on earth.

Most of my skin was either burnt or cut open like a fillet, exposing the white flesh underneath. My face was covered in blood and swollen, and I smelt like you'd expect if it were a fragrance. A smell reminiscent of ammonia, chared, and rotting flesh, mixing perfectly well with gasoline. My legs doubled in size as they swelled, filling themselves with blood. My hands were also swollen and looked cartoonish. Like I had on Mickey Mouse's large, puffy gloves. I resembled nothing as I did less than twenty minutes ago and was almost unrecognizable.

As the driver sat there, looking at me in the rearview mirror, I reached over his seat and slapped him on the side of his head. It was a light slap that was nonaggressive. One that I would give my little brother when my mom wasn't looking. I wanted to snap him out of the shock that he was in and focus on the mission. Unfortunately, we weren't out of the fight yet. We still had to retrieve our casualties and drive out of here with one less vehicle to return to base.

"Hey! Snap out of it and pass me the radio," I yelled at the driver.

After passing the radio's handset to me, I

called over our company's frequency so that anyone listening would hear. Unfortunately, the first two Humvees in our patrol had no idea what had taken place a few streets away from them. They were engaged with the enemy as much as we were, where they were located. If they knew how bad it was, I know they would have found a way to come back and help us.

"This is Spc. Avila. I have one killed in action, and possibly four wounded in action. Request an immediate medical evacuation. Over!" I shouted and pleaded over the radio.

There had been so much chaos in a brief period. I wasn't sure if anyone called in for a medivac. So, to be sure, I decided to call it in myself. If there's one thing that I've learned in war, it's to never underestimate the fog of war. With everything happening at once in the heat of a battle, soldiers can become confused and forgetful. Calling for a medivac was only to ensure that no one had forgotten.

After making the call and being treated by

the medic, I grabbed a nearby water bottle and poured it on my face. I needed something to cool me off and rinse the debris and blood from my eyes and body. The adrenaline dump I was on started to wear off, allowing some pain to settle again. I'm not sure if the medic saw me in the act of doing so, or he simply didn't know the repercussions I would face once I did. Although, I wish he had.

"Shit! My eyes!" I screamed out in pain. Nearly drowning myself in water made matters worse.

Water, mixed with the hazardous chemicals from the IED, flowed down my forehead and into my eyes. I couldn't see anything. It reminded me of my time in basic, after going through the gas chamber. A test that every soldier must pass before graduating. Enduring an enclosed room full of a few dozen new recruits and CS gas, commonly known as tear gas, for five minutes. The chemical's side effects include burning the eyes and skin. As well as an obscene amount of mucus discharge.

"You'll be fine, bro. I can't do anything

about your eyes right now. You'll have to fight through it until we get you back on base." The platoon medic said. My vision was the least of his concern, and my pain and discomfort weren't any of his problems. I had more critical injuries at the moment that needed his attention.

"Let's roll, boys!" SSG. Nuñes shouted, smacking the armored side of the Humvee as he jumped into the passenger seat.

I was relieved to finally be on our way out of here. So far, everything felt like I was stuck in a bad dream that I couldn't wake from. And making the call over the radio and giving a report of dead and wounded was a surreal moment for me. I wanted to be strong for the guys around me and keep my emotions suppressed as best I could. Despite the empty hole of sadness that I had growing inside.

The only thing I could think of on the ride back was the loss of Hartge. The emptiness that filled his eyes as I lay wounded in his lap was continuously repeated. It looped and replayed itself in my mind's eye repeatedly. While I had seen death before, that was the closest I had ever been. Nevertheless, I contributed as much as possible to the team and stayed in the fight. I felt that no one knew the streets of Adhamiyah as well as I did. So, I gave directions to our driver as best as possible with my limited visibility.

Thankfully, we made it back to our base without incident. Pulling through the large, metal gates at the entrance, I made one last call over the radio. Informing the medics waiting on our arrival which vehicles myself and the wounded were in. Without hesitation, our Humvee was swarmed by medics, who immediately got to work treating me. Each carried large bags full of medical gear. Far more than what we took on patrol.

The medical care provided on base was second to none. Here, we had access to licensed doctors and physicians who worked at the aid station. All of them were trained and backed by countless experiences in trauma care. Everything from gunshot wounds to soldiers with missing limbs. The medics at the aid station have seen it all. There wasn't a medical emergency that you could throw at them that they wouldn't be prepared to treat.

"How are you doing, soldier?" My platoon leader rushed over to ask as I was carried into the aid station. Leaning in as he asked, he had a sincere look that covered his facial features. One that a dad would have, asking his son if he was alright.

"Ain't nothin' but a chicken wing, sergeant!" I replied.

I couldn't have imagined how he must have felt, seeing a squad of his soldiers wounded and dead. He'd suffered enough as it was during this deployment with the loss of fourteen before today. Adding on to that number must have destroyed him. The role of the platoon leader in the army was more than a job or title. It entailed more than managing the younger enlisted soldiers that served under him. Instead, a platoon leader is likened to the father figure amongst the enlisted. One whose goal is to bring everyone back home safely and provide the necessary means. Failing to do such, and continuing the fight for the greater good of the mission, was a position I'm glad I didn't hold.

I knew I was in great hands while under the care of our medical staff and team. I suppose it was because of their care that I wasn't in as much pain as before. However, that all seemed to change once the medics rolled me into one of the triage rooms. Looking around at the stretchers next to me, I saw that Campos, Flemming, and Catterton were there as well. That's when it hit me. The pain I somehow held back reemerged and attacked me with a vengeance.

Seeing my brothers lying beside me and being treated was more than I could take. It was the first time we were together since I last saw them burning and on fire. I wasn't sure if they made it out alive and assumed the worse, even though I prayed for the best. I wished that I could have done more for them to prevent this from happening. As the gunner of our vehicle, who had a better view of the battlefield, I felt it was my responsibility to keep us safe on patrol.

"Morphine!" I reached up and grabbed one of the medics treating me, pulling him in close to ask if he could administer a shot of the pain-killing drug. The pain that I was experiencing became more than I could handle. I needed something to numb me. Otherwise, I felt that I was going to lose consciousness.

Shortly after injecting me with the powerful narcotic, I grabbed him and pulled him close once more. "If I die, it's not you," I whispered in his ear as the drug's effects kicked in. I didn't know what I meant at the time, and the medic chalked it up to simply being the drugs talking for me. Looking back, I suppose I was eluding that if I died in that room, he didn't have to carry the burden that he failed his mission to save my life. I knew that I was badly injured and had tasted death multiple times. If I were to succumb to my wounds, that was God's decision, and there wasn't anything or any drug that could prevent that from happening.

I faded in and out of consciousness while

being treated, making it hard to remember how much time elapsed. However, later that evening, I remember being awakened by one of the medics in the station. The medic came in and began preparing me to be transferred to the aid station in the green zone.

"We're going to get you out of here and better treatment, soldier. You'll be fine and on your way home in no time." He said, rebandaging and rewrapping my blood-soaked bandages.

Before I knew it, I was loaded into a medivac helicopter waiting on the landing pad near the aid station.

I guess this is it. I said to myself.

Despite the morphine running through my veins, I could still comprehend the gravity of what was happening. I knew that once I arrived at the green zone's aid station, it meant that I was on my way home. While receiving great medical care, my injuries were best treatable stateside. So there was no point in me staying in country. At least back home in the states, I had access to state-of-the-art technology with countless resources and support if needed.

I also understood that my war-fighting days would more than likely be coming to an end. The chances of me getting back into the fight, and rejoining my guys for another deployment, were slim. It hurt to come to this realization. But, I had to be honest with myself. My dream of getting payback and fighting for the country I loved was over. My only hope was that my guys knew that I did my best and that serving next to them was an honor I'll cherish for the rest of my life.

HAYLEE

"*I* understand how hard this must be for you, ma'am, and your family. I wish the chances were better than what they were. I'm sorry. I truly am. We're doing everything we can and will continue fighting for your son. However, with the type of injuries your son has suffered, there isn't much more we can do." While the doctor was saddened to be the bearer of bad news, he had to be honest with my mother.

"Chances? You mentioned that my son has a chance. What are they?" My mom asked.

"Well," The doctor took a brief pause, flipping and looking through handwritten and typed notes on his clipboard. "With everything that we were able to accomplish, and based on my assessment, I believe there is a thirty-three percent chance that your son survives his wounds."

Before the doctor could finish his sentence, my mom interrupted him, not wanting to hear another word he had to say. The doctors' odds of my survival were news she wouldn't allow herself to accept. Without her firstborn son, her future would be a reality she was unwilling to acknowledge.

"NO! I don't care about your percentage or chances! You don't know my son and the man that he is. You don't know him as I do." My mom asserted in a strong and definite tone. If there was anyone who knew who I was, from flesh to soul, it was my mother. At times, I believed she knew me better than I knew myself.

"Ma'am. I'm sorry to have to give you this unfortunate news. I truly am. As a doctor and someone who cares, I would advise that your family take time to talk to our chaplain and staff to help guide you through this process. They can also assist with getting your family in contact with someone for funeral arrangements. Again, I'm genuinely sorry. If I weren't completely honest with you, ma'am, I wouldn't be doing my job." He said, walking out of the room where my family gathered.

My mom, who mainly spoke with my primary doctor, fell silent. It seemed as if the words my doctor said were of a foreign language or his language had no meaning to her. Regardless of my survival odds, my mom knew they were incorrect with every fiber in her being. She believed that my chances of life were instead one-hundred percent. My mother thought it so much that she went as far as to ignore the advice of formally preparing for my death.

After the IED explosion and flying out of Iraq, I arrived in San Antonio', Texas, at the Brooke Army Medical Center. After my arrival, the doctors and nurses wasted little time doing what they could to save my life. If my injuries had happened a decade ago, I would haven't made it this far. Brooke Army Medical Center, BAMC, is the United States Army's premier medical institution. The

Army's largest medical center, BAMC, is the Department of Defense's only level 1 trauma center. So if there was a place that could treat and take care of me, BAMC was it.

Shortly after arriving at the medical center, doctors decided that placing me in a medically induced coma was best. While it may sound scary, medically induced comas have been a practice for over a quarter of a century. Its uses can serve in the treatment and care for multiple reasons. Critically ill patients, severe brain and head trauma, stroke victims, and seizures lasting longer than five minutes, to name a few. In my case, the trauma I suffered during the IED blast, placing me in a medically induced coma, was the best course of action to treat my injuries.

It was a state of awareness while in the hospital that I would spend three months of my life. While in a coma, the brain is essentially put in hibernation. In this state, it allows the brain time to heal and recuperate. I saw this medical procedure as something which allowed my brain to finally get some rest. However, there is a downside to a medical-induced coma, especially for patients suffering from traumatic brain injury. Undergoing the procedure, there was a risk a patient may never awaken. Or they could suffer long-lasting neurological negative side effects. Rather than my brain registering the pain I was constantly in and surgeries, my doctors felt that putting my brain to sleep was in my best interest.

While in a coma, unconscious, it's thought that an individual is unable to hear. And a patient only processes external stimuli to a small degree. This may be true, although it wasn't my experience. In fact, it was nearly the exact opposite. In a coma, I distinctly recall the voices of those around me. Likewise, I recognized some of the individuals I heard speaking nearby and could put a name to them.

The best description I can give, being in a coma, was similar to dreaming. A weird dream and something I haven't experienced since. One that consisted of no shapes or colors, depth or distance, and without dimension. Nothing. Instead, the space that I occupied was absolute darkness. It's what I'd imagine being lost in space would feel like. And, while in this dream world, a voice occasionally pierced through the darkness. Although, I couldn't distinguish where it originated or how far away the person was.

My family would visit me in the hospital and talk to me daily. Since arriving stateside, my family was there by my side. They would hold conversations, discuss their day, and give me words of encouragement. My mom, accompanied by my dad, typically prayed over me, sometimes for hours. My younger brother and sister talked about the events they were planning and told me how much they appreciated me as the big brother.

While in a coma, I heard their voices and knew who they were and their relationship to me. However, I was only able to comprehend fragments of what they discussed. Most of what I heard were certain names, phrases, and greetings. Nonetheless, I knew that my family was with me. If it weren't for them being there, I wouldn't have survived. Their dedication to faith and love allowed me to keep fighting and pull through.

Despite the odds I was given by the doctors, three months later, I was taken out of my induced coma. I wasn't sure how much time had passed when I came to. To my recollection, I was asleep for two, possibly three, days. I was shocked that so much time had elapsed, and I wasn't aware of it. However, not as stunned as the doctors who greeted me when I awoke and showed promising signs of a successful recovery.

It was good to be back. Alive and surrounded by family and those who cared. There wasn't anything that I could have wanted or asked for. Yet, during a time when everyone should be rejoiceful, it was difficult not to shake off the sadness that I was feeling. Shortly after coming out of the coma, I wanted to know how my guys were doing. The last news that I remembered was that other than Hartge, everyone else in my vehicle, despite third-degree burns, all survived.

Eighteen days after the incident, while at BAMC, Campos succumbed to his wounds. He arrived at the medical facility at the same time I had and continued fighting like hell. I was devastated to learn of the news and had difficulty processing it. If it weren't for him reaching back and grabbing me in the Humvee, I wouldn't be here. Campos sacrificed his life so that I could be here today, which was a debt I could never repay. I owed my brother in arms more than life or anything I could offer. And, for that, I am eternally thankful. In my eyes, Campos was the true hero on that day, May 14, 2007.

A long, tough, rocky road ahead of me at BAMC. More than seventy percent of my body had been burned. Most of the burns that the IED caused were third-degree and destroyed a large portion of my skin. My right side suffered the most damage. My back, legs, hands, and face all required various surgeries, skin grafts, and reconstruction.

I knew my journey toward recovery would be challenging, but there was nothing that could prepare me for what was ahead. My right foot would need to be removed before eventually progressing to an amputation from below the knee. I lost the function of my fingers and underwent the painful process of removing scar tissue in large areas of my body. The doctors were able to save one role in my hand. When asked if there was anything I couldn't live without, I told the doctors that being able to shoot was something I enjoyed and wanted to continue. So, instead of removing my fingers on my right hand, they fused my index and middle together so that I could pull a weapon trigger. A procedure I'm grateful for and continue to use today.

The surgeries and work the doctors had to perform seemed endless. After the surgeries, rehabilitation, and being reduced to a room, I was ready to finally leave. I had spent so much time in the confined space I was willing to do anything to get out. Finally, after seventy surgeries, my wishes were granted. While I would not be fully discharged and out-processed from the facility, I was moved to a more private location near the main hospital.

Across the street, in the medical center, were housing units provided and funded by Fisher House for patients and their families. Like apartments, the housing provided a location and environment that allowed soldiers to heal with the comfort of being home. A home away from home. My mom, dad, sister, and brother would visit throughout the day and attend my rehab appointments. When my family had to leave for the day, my mother stayed behind and took care of me.

Due to my injuries, I was unable to take care of myself. Even though I was out of the immediate supervision of the doctors and nurses, I still needed help and someone to watch over me. I lost most of the function in my muscles, my leg was amputated, and my scars and wounds bleed often. In addition, I had to relearn simple tasks I once took for granted as if I had never done them before. Tying my shoe, washing my face, and walking, would take me months to learn again.

Every day in recovery, I thought about how

one singular event changed my life forever. I wasn't the same after the IED. I dreamt about it nearly every night and was forced to see it whenever I saw myself in the mirror. The young man, in my reflection, wasn't the tall, twenty-one-year-old soldier built like a linebacker I once knew. Instead, I lost over forty pounds since the incident and shrank to the size of a high school tennis player. The burns killed most of my body's muscles, making lifting the smallest object feel like an Olympic-sized weight. And to make matters worse, I had to rely on my mom to help me use the restroom.

The independent, strong warfighter I became wasn't represented well by my physical appearance and reliance on others to function. I felt like I had become a burden on my family. Especially my mother. Her having to bathe me and see me when I was most vulnerable crushed me. I knew she didn't expect that after everything she's been through, she would be wiping her adult son's ass.

Some days were tougher than others. There were mornings I felt like I could take on the entire world and had the motivation to make the best of my situation. Then, some days, I felt like I was a complete failure. There wasn't anything anyone could say that would change my way of thinking. On bad days, I thought that I had failed my teammates and let them down for not being there with them. The war in Iraq was reaching peak fighting season, and I wasn't there to contribute. Not being able to make my family proud by serving my country and making something of myself, I also believed I failed them.

I gave up my pursuit of being a professional football player. Instead, deciding to stand up for my country and those who couldn't. After September 11, I promised myself that I would do everything possible to get revenge for our country. But, now, in the state that I was in, I couldn't even defend myself.

All that I trained to become seemed like it were all for nothing. Years of training and what I experienced in the war didn't mean anything if I couldn't even put on my own pants and lace up my boots. At least in combat, I had a purpose. I could take care of and fight for myself. One task needed to be accomplished, and that was killing the enemy. It's what I was growing to become good at. Besides sports, being a US soldier was the only thing I excelled in, and I had a sense of fulfillment.

I had nothing but time on my hands when I wasn't attending physical therapy or undergoing another surgery. Perhaps, too much time. So I sat in my room, thinking about all the things that could have happened. I went over countless outcomes if situations were to have played out differently than they had. Maybe I would have progressed in my military career and sought out new, more challenging goals. If there was a possibility that I could have done something differently on patrol, that would have ultimately prevented Campos's death.

There was a spiderweb of countless possible realities I formed. Each strand of the silky web representing all the things I could, would, and should have done differently. I went from being confined to a small hospital room to being trapped in the prison I created in my mind. Similar to my train of thought while flying to Iraq. Faced with the reality of who I saw in the mirror, I couldn't shake the mental state that I was in.

Waking up every day, hoping to get better, slowly faded. As crazy as it may seem, I felt the world would be better if I didn't exist in it. Removing myself from the lives of others, who I've become a burden, would make life easier for everyone. I wouldn't be forced to see my mom suffer because I couldn't care for myself. Or feel that I was a family member who didn't live up to the expectations I set forth for me.

I felt responsible for missing out on the life that continued outside the parameter of the hospital. I missed family birthday parties and sharing moments of excitement with each other. Being unable to watch my brother and sister graduate and walk across the stage to receive their diploma hurt. Hell, I couldn't even attend my brother's funeral or be there for him as he lay dying in the same hospital as me. What was the point of living if I couldn't witness or experience it?

My thoughts became like a deadly infection that destroyed my spirit. Negative thoughts became the only thing that filled my mind. Finally, after months of continuing with the same mundane routine, waking up, attending treatments and therapy, and a relentless cycle of pain, I wanted it to end. Every small progression I had in physical therapy seemed to always take two steps in the opposite direction. There was more to life than this, and I knew it.

Even if I could live somewhat of a normal life, some stipulations came with it. Such as never being able to run the way I used to or driving. Putting my clothes on or going out to eat without someone staring at me because of how I looked. The life that I was used to and how I would be perceived by others, including myself, have permanently changed. Life was going to be an entirely new experience, with pain accompanying me for the rest of my life.

Finally, one day with no difference from any other, I no longer wanted to continue the fight I dealt with. My outlook on life and my role in it diminished entirely. I've come close to this feeling in the past. However, on this day, I broke and came crashing down into the pit of sadness I had created. Survivor's guilt, remorse, shame, and a plethora of emotions sandwiched and smashed together,

Looking back, I suppose my mom knew I was struggling emotionally. To the best of my knowledge, I didn't display any signs that I was in a dark place. I envisioned myself as being someone who hid their emotions quite well. Someone who didn't wear my heart on their sleeve. Usually, I kept how I felt tucked inside when going through hard times. I would place my emotions, the ones that made me vulnerable, in an imaginary box and store them until they would eventually dissolve away.

While I sat at the foot of my bed, my mind was made up on my decision. I wanted to kill myself. That's as simple and plain as it could be. I didn't want to feel anything at this point. Forever being numb to the emotions that swirled within me. Removing myself from this long equation called life was the best way I could rationalize my situation. While the thought of suicide had crossed my mind before, this was the first time I took any action on it.

I had everything set in place. I spent the morning planning when, where, and how I would take my own life. Telling my family or leaving anything behind was out of the question. I was already a hassle to them. So, I didn't want to bother them more than I needed.

In the army, I was taught that the easiest way to neutralize a threat was to kill it. Without its existence, it was impossible to cause further harm, thus allowing the mission to continue. In my case, I was the threat. I was a threat to not only myself but to those around me, forced to alter their lives to accommodate mine. I felt I knew what needed to occur for the success of others to continue and thrive.

I was at peace with my decision to take my own life. After all that I had been through, death didn't scare me as much as it used to. The loss of my brothers, still fighting overseas, would make it easier for me to carry through with the act. Hoping that once on the other side, I will see them again.

"Omar. Son, I hope you know you are loved." My mom said, peeking her head into my room before making her way over to sit next to me. "I want you to understand that your family will always love you no matter what. There isn't anything you could do to change that for any of us." She continued. "You've made all of us proud at what you've done. Your brother and sister really look up to you a lot. In fact, you're all that they ever seem to talk about. There isn't a day that passes; they don't talk about how proud they are to have you as a big brother. You don't have to worry about me, either. I'm your mother, and this is what a mother's job is. To take care of their children. No matter how old or what you become in life, you

were and always will be my son first and foremost."
I hadn't said a word or interrupted her the entire
time she spoke to me.

"Omar, do you remember touching your
niece for the first time?" My mother asked. She was
referring to my brother's fiance, who carried my
unborn niece in her belly. Since joining the army
and deploying, my younger brother met the love of
his life and began creating a family for himself.
Between training, being stationed in Germany, and
the hustle and bustle of army life, it was hard to
keep up and visit family as much as I would have
liked. Being back in the states was the first time I'd
seen them together, with their baby on the way.

While I was in a coma, my brother and his
fiance would place my hand on her stomach to feel
their baby kicking and moving. I didn't have any
recollection of it taking place. Although, my family
saw and believed otherwise. According to my
mom's accounts, I moved and responded each time
they placed my hand on my unborn niece.

Hearing my mom speak of my reaction

while in a coma put me in a difficult situation. On the one hand, I wrestled with the idea of ending my life. While on the other hand, I couldn't bear not being here for the birth of my niece. I found it odd yet remarkable that someone I hadn't met could affect me in such a way. A spirit that I bonded with, full of life, and had a wonderful, bright future ahead.

While listening to my mom talk with me about my niece and how often we informally met, the more my connection to her grew. And as she continued, I realized how much my mother allowed me to take a step back from the mental ledge I was standing on. Even if it were only for a second, it gave me the time to consider the future of others. How my actions would affect the lives of others, regardless if I met them or not.

My niece was going to be my parents' first grandchild. While she wasn't my own kid, I wanted to be there for her and witness all of her accomplishments. Having a new member join our family, I suppose, resurfaced the big brother that was still inside me. My newborn niece wouldn't care what I looked like or could do. I knew that being in her future was all that mattered.

After listening to my mom, without her knowing the intentions, I had that day, I decided against acting on them. Instead, I decided to give life a chance and continue my mission. To complete my therapy and be in my nieces' life.

With the birth of my niece approaching quickly, I made a promise to myself. I swore that I would be there to hold her. Unfortunately, due to my therapy scheduling, I couldn't be there the day she was born. However, I wanted to meet her as soon as I could. I owed that to her. While she didn't know, I believe it was because of her that I could get out of my slump. She was the only person who could cause me to move when I lay in a coma. I owed it to her to be there soon after she entered the world.

I asked my doctor what it would take for me to see my niece after she was born. Unfortunately, the medical staff wouldn't allow a newborn in the room to see me. The risk of contracting an illness in an environment where various diseases and infections reside was very high. So instead, the doctors presented me with an option that would benefit everyone. If I could walk unaided to the visitor's room, I could see her there.

It would take months to regain the strength I needed to be able to complete the walk. Less than three hundred feet from my room to the visitor's area wasn't a great distance. But on the other hand, walking from my bed to the restroom seemed like a marathon. Building the strength I needed to make the stroll would take every ounce of my dedication and what was left in my reserve tanks. Nevertheless, I was willing to endure whatever it took to see and hold my newborn niece.

I was constantly reminded by the pain in therapy that my path ahead wasn't easy or for the faint-hearted. The only thing that kept me going, and pushing through the pain, was meeting my niece. My brother and his fiance agreed and settled on a name for the newest member of our tribe.

Haylee. According to an online search, Haylee has several meanings. Though it has a Norse origin, meaning hero. Without meeting my niece, I already knew who she was. My hero. Regardless if she or her parents knew it. She gave me hope again, saving my life.

I continued treatment, and day by day, my muscles grew stronger. However, getting used to my new leg, a prosthetic, was challenging and took some time. It was the hardest thing I had ever done physically and mentally. More so than basic training or anything Iraq threw at me while I was deployed. But, Haylee was the strength and boost I needed to see myself through.

Then, a moment I once thought impossible became a reality. Finally, I could walk under my own will after hours, weeks, and months of practice and consistency. And, I could do so unassisted for the three hundred feet my doctor requested. While the accomplishment didn't seem like a big deal to some, it meant the world to me. It's something that I could see through to the end, despite my physical limitations. An accomplishment that allowed me to know that despite my condition, anything was achievable. So long as I put my mind to the task and didn't allow myself to quit.

Soon, a few weeks after Haylee's birth, I could finally meet her in person. The sweat, tears, and blood I spilled came to this moment. My brother and his fiance were waiting for me with their newborn baby girl inside the visitors center.

"You've got this, big bro!"

"This is all you, Omar!"

My family shouted, cheering me on as I sat in my wheelchair from across the street. Even though I could hear their encouragement, my focus was on Haylee.

Standing and gaining my balance, I began to walk toward her. I was a bit shaky at first, and the pain shooting through my leg was mind-numbing. So much so that, halfway there, I questioned if I would make it without taking a break or falling over.

One more step. One more step. Just one more step. I

repeated to myself, over and over. Until finally, I was standing in front of my beautiful baby niece. My brother placed her in my arms, congratulating me. The emotions that ran through me are feelings I'll never be able to fully and truly express. This innocent child, full of life and potential, was responsible for this moment, and she hadn't the slightest idea.

Standing there, holding Haylee in my arms, seemingly voided all the pain I was in as if it didn't exist. Something so fragile and small made one of the greatest impacts on my life. I didn't say much to her, as I only managed to stare in amazement and thankfulness. Haylee was my reason for fighting to live, and it began when I was in a coma, with neither of us knowing that the other existed.

I went from wanting to fight for the revenge of my country to fighting to live. In one instance, I was trained and prepared for battle by professional soldiers I hold in high regard. On the other hand, the fight for my life was made possible by the innocence of a child. A stark contrast between the two. While I'm thankful for both experiences, only one has allowed me to see the light in one of my darkest moments. Thank you, Haylee. Your uncle Omar loves you and will be here to see all the great things you do.

LEGEND

*B*orn in 1974 in the small town of Odessa,

Texas, a young, energetic kid had no clue he was destined to become a legend. After graduating from high school in 1992 and attending a state university for a couple of years, this young man would enlist in the military. The United States Navy. Then, by age twenty-five, he excelled in the ranks, becoming a United States Navy SEAL sniper.

The enemy referred to him as "The Devil of Ramadi" after his ninety-one kills operating in that city. This sniper was so effective at his job, killing the enemy and saving American lives, that the enemy placed a bounty on his head. A twenty thousand dollar reward for his killing or capture.

The Navy SEAL sniper continued to deploy to Iraq, working in Baghdad, Ramadi, and Fallujah. After ten years of service to his country, he left the military with more than one hundred and fifty kills to his name. The most recorded kills for a US sniper in combat. A record that still stands today.

His name is Chris Kyle. A carrier of the Silver Star and four Bronze Star Medals for valor. After the military, Chris struggled to transition to civilian life and his relationship with his family. Having difficulty finding his purpose in life, he became an entrepreneur. In 2009, Chris founded and started his company, Craft International. It was a security company that provided training services, such as long-range shooting, to military members.

Unfortunately, in 2013, Kyle and his friend were shot and murdered. Not on the battlefields of Iraq or Afghanistan; instead, they died here, in the United States. Shot to death by one of their own. A veteran. The two men were killed on a shooting range in Texas, doing what they loved most. Helping other veterans returning from combat and who struggled with post-traumatic stress.

Kyles's history in the military and what he has accomplished far exceeds mine, and our careers couldn't be more opposite. Chris was a Navy SEAL. A special operations unit that is arguably considered the toughest within the military. I was an infantryman in the army. I had no specialties, and my team wasn't tasked with handling classified high-threat operations.

Someone of Kyle's caliber is someone I wouldn't expect to meet or care anything about me. However, we met face-to-face and had the opportunity to talk. Despite the differences in our military achievements, Chris helped me in a way no doctor has been able to. And did so, in the least likely of places, with medicine I was never prescribed.

Growing up in an immigrant family, going out for a hunt wasn't our priority. Instead, we focused on working, providing food for the family, and a roof over our heads. As a result, there wasn't much time for hunting after work or on the weekends. With my dad's busy schedule with work, taking a rifle out in the woods to harvest a deer wasn't a hobby we could entertain. But, the idea of it intrigued me.

I remember overhearing some of my classmates talk about their hunting experiences in middle school. Listening to their stories with their fathers, uncles, and brothers, I was admittedly envious of them. They had fun in the woods, hunting deer, wild pigs, or turkey for harvest. I wanted to know what it felt like to have those memories with their dad. After hearing how it made them feel and the excitement in their voice, I promised myself. When I was old enough and could afford the time, I would find time to go hunting.

Unfortunately, hunting was furthest from my radar after deploying and being wounded. I was either recovering from surgery, healing, or attending physical therapy. It made it almost impossible to ever find the time to venture off for a hunt. Shooting was something that I've enjoyed since joining the army; however, it wasn't of pressing concern.

Suffering the types of injuries I had, recovery was a long road. I describe it as a marathon race rather than a sprint's fast pace. In fact, the process of healing may never end. Instead, it's a lifelong process. So understandably, some moments were made possible that I felt sorry for myself.

Some days were, of course, harder than others. There were moments I didn't feel like getting out of bed to start the day or go to one of my treatments. On other days, I felt like a one-man army, ready to overcome whatever obstacles I faced. Then there were terrible days. I thought I was on my last leg (no pun intended) and didn't know if I had the strength to mentally carry on.

The memories from my IED blast never faded. I thought about my guys daily and wondered how everything was going overseas. But, the war for the guys I deployed with didn't stop after I left, and their military careers progressed. Sometimes I wondered how different things would be if I wasn't injured and forced to leave the army. I missed my brothers in arms. Especially those who didn't make it back home alive.

I was dealing with a ton of emotions after my time in service. Often, I struggled with how to best deal with them. But, I knew life could be an enjoyable experience. The issue I had, was finding the assistance to guide me in that direction. I've talked with doctors and therapists and shared what I was going through with them. Some recommended medication to help cope, to get me out of the frame of mind I sometimes fell into. Other recommendations were experimental and didn't seem to help me much.

I was beginning to think that the mental scars of war would never heal. I imagined post-traumatic stress as a lasting condition and a side effect of combat. While it wasn't something I wanted to live with for the rest of my life, I would understand if that were the case. I knew what I signed up for. To fight for and serve my country. There were no guarantees that I would come out unscathed. But, if fighting for my country and mental scars went hand in hand together, it's a sacrifice I would still make today.

"Hey, bro! Long time, no talk. If you're not too busy next week, how'd you like to come out and hunt with us?" One of my friends I met while staying at BAMC asked on the other end of the phone. After I left the medical center, we fell out of touch due to our schedules, and I hadn't spoken with him since.

"Hell yes! You can count me in." I responded.

I needed to get out of my house. Being couped up by myself for long durations of time, I wasn't at my best mentally. So while it was unexpected, he couldn't have called at a more perfect time. I was excited to fulfill my childhood dream of hunting. Even if it weren't with my dad, it would be with someone I deeply connected with. Getting around like-minded individuals who have been through similar experiences as I was what I needed.

After hanging up the phone, I remember hopping in my truck and driving to the nearest sporting goods store. I had a rifle that I bought a few days ago, although I lacked the necessary essentials for hunting in the woods. I grabbed a backpack and began stocking it with water bottles, snacks, gloves, face paint, camouflage pants, and shirts. I was so new to the hobby that the camo patterns I bought didn't match. The pants were for blending in with one environment and terrain, while the shirts were for another.

I felt an excitement that I hadn't experienced in a long time. It was like I was a kid again, the night before waking up to presents on Christmas day. The evening before my first hunting trip, I packed my bags and what I would wear laid out and ready to go. I remember going over in my head what I would do and how I was going to react if I shot a deer. It's been some time since I've fired a rifle, and I couldn't wait to have that feeling again.

After preparing for the hunt, I decided to go to bed early that night. I knew I had a long drive ahead and needed the rest. A lack of sleep wouldn't be why I missed out on an experience that's been in the making for over a decade. However, falling asleep wouldn't be as easy as I imagined. Not because I was excited or had jitters of anticipation. Rather, it was a lack of self-esteem and self-pity.

You see, I wasn't very comfortable with myself at the time. I had yet to accept who I was and how others may view me. I struggled with who I was and had become. It was hard to cope with my injuries and the marks and scars that covered my body. I used a prosthetic leg and lost a ton of weight. I looked nothing like I used to. I was still getting used to my new attributes.

As I lay in bed, I slowly started to talk myself out of going on the hunting trip. Who I was, I wondered how I would be excepted by others. I felt like an outsider. All these emotions began taking over my better judgment, talking me out of going. I wrestled with the ideas, juggling both in my mind, unsure of what I would do.

The next morning, as the sun rose, I still tendered between the options and remained undecided.

"*Just stay in bed. At least here, no one will judge us. Here, at home, we're safe. No one can look at us differently here. C'mon. Just stay home.*" I told myself, searching for any excuse not to go.

Then, I heard it. That voice again. It was the same voice I heard while burning inside my

Humvee, laying on top of Hartge's body. The one that came from within and convinced me to keep fighting.

"Dude, just get up. Get the hell up! What's the worst thing that can happen? Someone thinks something negative of you, or you get uncomfortable. So what? Who cares? You get back in your truck and leave. It wouldn't be the worst thing that's happened to you."

I took my better half's advice and decided to make the trip. So, with my rifle in hand, bags packed and carrying everything I needed, I got in my truck and left. The decision came at the last moment, with little time to spare. Not even time to grab something to eat or a cup of coffee.

The drive was uneventful and went as I had planned. My journey began near the suburbs and city limits before entering the open country fields of East Texas. I remember thinking how beautiful the scenery was. So much so that I found myself paying more attention to mother nature than I did keeping my eyes on the road. It was a feeling that I hadn't felt in some time. Peace.

Nearing the ranch where we would be hunting, I was taken back by how serene it was there. There weren't tall buildings or shopping centers. No sounds of early morning rush hour traffic or commercial planes flying overhead. Other than birds chirping and the noises of wind rustling the leaves on the trees, the area was silent. A silence that, initially, took some time to adjust to.

After pulling into the front gates of the ranch, I made my way toward a large cabin, where everyone met. A radiant cabin that looked like it could have been featured on a holiday postcard. I walked up a graveled driveway and stood two large, hardwood French doors toward the main door. Before I had the chance to knock, the door peeled open, and I was greeted by someone standing in the opening.

A young man, missing both legs, and one arm, stood there.

"Welcome, brother! Come on in!" He shouted as he waved me in with a grin stretching from one ear to the other. The excitement in his expression let me know that he was having a hell of a great time.

He was a fellow brother in arms. A fellow wounded soldier. A small commotion of people laughing and conversing carried on behind him. Nearly everyone in the open-spaced reception area had an ice-cold beer and a smile. It felt good to be around the positive energy that filled the room.

I was taught a valuable lesson early on, walking in with the soldier who greeted me. This guy looked like me. He suffered some of the same wounds as me. If not more. And he's witnessed the same bloodshed on the same battlefields I've fought in. Yet, here he was, smiling and laughing, talking with people he's never met. He wasn't allowing his issues and injuries to control him.

The wounded soldier didn't have a care in the world about what others thought of him. He could care less if someone looked at him with a face of disgust or what they thought of his injuries. His outlook on life wasn't determined by what he saw in the mirror. It was the heavy dose of perspective that I needed. Never let my circumstances decide who I want to be. It could always be worse.

I was one of the last guys attending the hunt to arrive at the ranch. Most of everyone here came a few hours ago and got acquainted. I made myself around the room, introducing myself and having a beer. It felt good to be around people again. I was tucking myself in my house for so long that I forgot how much I missed socializing.

The time on our watches approached midnight. Hours of talking and sharing stories flew by in an instant. Then, as we all conversed over cold drinks, the ranch owner walked into the reception to introduce himself and give us the details for the hunt.

"Good evening, gentleman! First, I want to thank you all for what you have done and for taking the time to be here. I see a couple of new faces here, so I want to personally give a warm welcome to you." The owner paused and looked in my direction with a welcoming smile before continuing. "I know you're all having a good time; however, we have a hunt in a few hours. I plan to take you guys out for some excitement in the blinds at six o'clock in the morning. If we're lucky, we'll tag us some whitetail, so plan accordingly."

As the owner left the reception area, everyone else slowly began making their way to their rooms in the cabin. Rather than grab some shut-eye, I opted to stay up for a bit and have another drink. Perhaps to soak in the amazing time I was already having. Sitting by myself at a long, hardwood, rectangular table, a tall individual wearing a ball cap with a skull patch logo walked over and sat in front of me.

"Hey, how you doin' man? I'm Chris." He said, with a thick country accent behind a large pinch of a dip in his bottom lip.

"Hey brother, I'm Omar," I responded.

Chris reached down and pulled his hand out from underneath the table. He held a handle of Tennessee whiskey, placed it on the table, and slid it in front of me.

"Would you like a nightcap?" He asked.

"Absolutely! Hell yes, I would. Pour me a shot!"

Chris and I talked with one another and got to know each other. The only pause in our conversation was to take another shot of whiskey. He came across as a really nice guy. One who genuinely listened. Only wanting to have a good time. He didn't talk much about his military service. The most Chris mentioned was that he once served in the Navy and deployed a few times.

Then, before I knew it, I saw that we had drunk half the bottle. I knew that Navy guys could drink. However, I knew that Chris had done this before and could keep going. We continued talking, mostly about where we grew up, sports and life. Soon, when the bottle of whiskey was almost finished, Chris's attitude changed. Not in a bad way, as in a drunken rage. Instead, a seriousness, which I hadn't seen since we started talking.

"How are you doin'?" Chris asked, looking directly into my eyes.

"I'm great," I said.

Though I meant what I said, I was fine; that wasn't what Chris referred to.

"No. How are you doing?" This time, when he asked, he leaned in toward me while tapping his temple on the side of his head. Gesturing that, he was instead inquiring about my mental state.

I never mentioned my injuries or how I got them throughout our conversation. Chris didn't ask. Besides, I wasn't comfortable talking about what I was going through with anyone else. My wounds were still fresh, and I was encountering a few dark patches in my life from time to time. I didn't have the charisma back then that I carry today. Someone willing to talk with anyone about what happened to me in Iraq.

Rather than refraining from talking with Chris, I opened up. For the first time, I talked about what I was going through, how it affected me, and who I was. At first, it was like peeling back the scabs on my body and revealing them to someone I had never met. But then, slowly, those wounds and scars I shared with Chris became less painful.

"You know those demons you're fighting; you don't have to fight them alone, brother." Chris sincerely said to me. I knew he meant it by the tone in his voice and the look in his eyes, and he didn't come across as someone who said things just to say them. "You don't have to fight them alone. That's why we're all here. One fight, one team. And if we stick together, then we can get through this." He continued.

Right then and there, listening to Chris, I realized something. I was not in this alone. On this hunting trip, mostly wounded veterans, the guys here were fighting the same demons I was. Some of them faced greater battles than I had. We needed to have each other's back. While the severity of our wounds varied, we were all fighting for the same thing.

Before I knew it, the sun was beginning to come over the horizon. I guess losing track of time is a side effect of good conversation amongst good people. Then, everyone asleep began making their way out of their rooms and into the reception area where Chris and I were sitting.

"Have you guys been up all night?" My friend, who invited me on the trip, asked?

"Sure have!" I replied.

"Are you guys planning on hunting?"

"Definitely, I wouldn't want to miss it. We'll sleep when we're done hunting." I laughed.

Chris and I rushed to our rooms and quickly dressed. After grabbing everything I needed for the hunt and back into the reception area, one of the guys stopped me.

"Dude, you were talking with Chris Kyle all night?" he asked.

"Uh…Yeah." His question confused me. I wondered if it were a bad thing or if I wasn't supposed to talk with him.

"Do you know who that is?"

"Yeah. Chris." I replied, still confused.

"No, dude. Do you know who Chris is?"

"I guess not. Who is he?"

"Bro, that's Chris Kyle. The Navy SEAL

who's the deadliest sniper in US history. Over a hundred fifty kills. Dude's a legend." He continued, informing me of Chris's accolades and accomplishments.

Learning who Chris was, made me respect him that much more. While I already viewed him as a pretty cool guy, Chris, never mentioning what he's done, spoke volumes. Here's someone, who's accomplished more than I could ever have imagined, and he never once bragged. Instead, Chris only cared about how I was and what he could do to help me through it. For that and his concern, I'm extremely grateful.

Once Chris was dressed and back in the reception area, he looked over and pointed at me.

"You and me, we're going hunting together." He said. There wasn't anything that I could do about it, nor did I want to. Chris picked me to hunt with him, and that was final.

After making our way out of the cabin and into the woods, Chris and I found a suitable blind we could shoot from. Once inside, we had a one hundred and eighty-degree unobstructed view through three slots on the sides and front. The scenery was beautiful. The sun's rays beamed on the ground, causing a misty haze to rise. And the sounds of serenity and peace permitted the atmosphere around us.

Me, Chris, and my rifle. That's all that seemed to matter. *Damn, it feels good to be out here.* I said to myself. It's been so long since I've felt this kind of peacefulness and quiet. Not only outside but inside as well.

"Deer!" Chris whispered excitedly and quietly, trying not to alarm the animal.

"Where?"

"Dude, it's right over there in front of you."

"I see it!" I responded back with the same excitement and enthusiasm.

Some time had passed, sitting in the blind in nearly complete quietness, before Chris spotted our first deer to enter our line of sight. It took me a few moments to spot the deer, which blended well with the environment. It was a six-point buck, standing broadside, less than one hundred yards from our blind. And we were going to take it.

I was going to be the one to take the shot, as Chris suggested. So, slowly, I raised my rifle. Shouldering the buttstock before finally settling my crosshairs on the deers' side. Just behind the shoulder blade. Hitting him in that area would be an instant kill and prevent the animal from suffering.

Initially, the shot seemed to be an easy one. I've been overseas before and had living targets in front of my sight. Plus, one hundred yards was something I knew I could accomplish in my sleep. While I wasn't a sniper, I had to hit targets at three times the distance the deer stood from us to graduate basic training. Little did I know, my first time shooting a deer was entirely different than I expected.

Hunters often refer to it as Buck Fever. That's what I had as I was about to take the shot. It strikes the best of hunters, regardless of their experience hunting game. Nervousness and shortness of breath, Buck Fever caused me to shake and my crosshairs to jump and move sporadically, making the shot more difficult than it needed to be.

"Take a deep breath, and breathe, brother. Put your sights on him, relax, and pull the trigger. It's just you and me out here. You got this." Chris instructed.

Moments later, relaxing as much as possible, I pulled the trigger. The deer suddenly dropped in its place.

"Ahhh! Yeah!"

"Hell yes!"

We both erupted in excitement, no longer needing to remain silent.

"Bro, this is awesome! That's my first deer!" I shouted at Chris.

"What? That's your first? That's freakin awesome, man. Why didn't you tell me this was your first deer?" He asked, giving me a high five.

"Yeah, that's my first one. I've always wanted to hunt since I was a kid." I replied.

"Omar, we're definitely going to do

something special for you. Let's get over and check it out."

Chris led me to where the deer was lying and checked it to ensure it was a good shot and dead. Then, reaching down and wiping his hand in its blood before smearing it on my face. An act that dates back to the eighteenth century amongst the hunting community to welcome newcomers to the hunting ranks.

This singular experience changed my life and how I went on to perceive it. Simply put, it was epic. Being here was more than I could have asked for and everything that I needed. But, it wasn't the act of killing or finally fulfilling a childhood dream. Instead, it was everything else. It was getting out of my comfort zone and experiencing life and the great outdoors. Being here was the best, most gratifying, and long-lasting medicine no doctor or therapist has ever prescribed. Its only side effects are memories I'll cherish for the rest of my life.

---- A Few Months Later ----

In 2010, three years after being wounded in Iraq, I was given the opportunity of a lifetime. One that I'm sure a lot of wounded veterans could benefit from. After my hunting adventure with the Legend, Chris Kyle, I shortly found myself back in Iraq. However, my mission would be much different during this trip and wouldn't involve killing the enemy. Instead, my objective was to heal. It was also to help shed insight on my experience with my fellow brothers and sisters in arms after being wounded in combat.

I didn't return to the same place that had taken so much from me of my free will. Instead, like much of what I've done in life, it was with the help and encouragement of others. Those who wanted to see me improve and return to the old me before the burns and scars.

During my hospital tenure, recovering from

my wounds, I was met by two gentlemen, Rick Kell and David Feherty. These two men were the founders of the non-profit organization Troops First Foundation, which organized the program Operation Proper Exit. Both would often visit the hospitals with veterans severely wounded in combat and offer their organization's services to help in the healing process of those recovering.

Operation Proper Exit is a unique organization, unlike any others in what they offer. Their goal is simple. Help wounded warfighters who are thriving in their recovery return to the theater in which they were wounded. And in 2010, with the help of Rick and David, I was afforded this rare opportunity. I would not only return to the country where I was wounded, but to the exact location, my injuries took place.

Initially, I was what you could expect. Nervous. I wasn't sure what to expect or if I was ready to return to the place I once referred to as hell. But, at the same time, I wanted questions that kept me up at night to finally be answered. I wanted to know if what we did in Iraq was all we could have done. In particular, I wanted to see for myself that there wasn't anything I could have done differently to change the tragic outcome the day we encountered the IED.

The entire trip with Operation Proper exit was a week-long trip in Iraq. Over the week, I would attend various bases and engage with the soldiers, discussing my experiences after the injury. My talks were in the form of a town hall meeting, able to answer questions anyone may have had regarding my transition and healing process. I didn't know what to expect, being amongst my brothers and sisters in my capacity. But it didn't take long to realize how much impact it had on me, able to help and offer my assistance. All without ever having to fight next to them, engaging the enemy in close combat.

After touring a few bases and speeches, my week ended with a visit to the scene where I was injured. I'll never forget the raw, unfiltered emotions that ran through me as I boarded the helicopter for the flight out. I didn't have a clue what to expect. The last time I was in the area, it seemed like the world was ending, and all hell had broken loose. I wasn't sure if the site was still as violent or if there was still a presence of the enemy lurking around. I wasn't carrying a rifle or hand grenades to defend myself even if we were engaged. I had to put my trust in the helicopter crew and the soldiers that have been keeping their boots on the enemy's throat.

While short in duration, the flight out was one of the most nerve-racking flights of my life. It also put me in an uncomfortable feeling of vulnerability. Regardless, I knew that this once-in-a-lifetime opportunity was one that a select few had the chance to experience. And because of that, I knew I had to take a moment for what it was worth and take it all in. This would be my chance to put the nail in the coffin and seal off any negative thoughts that I could have done more to alter what happened that day in 2007.

As we approached the site of the IED blast,

I felt my heart pounding against my chest as if it wanted to burst out and run for cover. My senses were overloaded as if I were back on a mission, and the environment quickly became familiar to me once again. Although, the presence of enemy fighters was nowhere to be found. In fact, it appeared as if they never existed. It was like the infestation of terrorists plaguing the region had been completely wiped out. Which, more than likely, was the case. Given the relentless pursuit and destruction of the enemy, our forces continued after my time in the country.

The view of the town streets below hadn't drastically changed. And, I could still identify the roads I had traveled a few years prior from two hundred feet in the air.

Damn…How did we make it out of here alive? I silently thought to myself. I was in complete silence. My eyes were laser-focused on the narrow street below where the IED detonated and struck my Humvee. Before arriving at the site, everything I was initially worried about suddenly seemed to vanish. The only thing that mattered was confined to that small area in the Iraqi street as we circled above. I wanted to take it all in. I wanted to relive the chaotic scene, moment by moment, play by play.

As we continued to circle the site for a few moments, the answers I needed slowly began revealing themselves to me. From my birdseye view and at that moment, I knew that there wasn't anything we could have done differently in 2007. We were surrounded, outnumbered, and wounded. Given the circumstances of that day, it's surprising that we didn't suffer many more casualties. From a couple of hundred feet in the air, I relived, saw, and knew we did all we could and fought our hardest that day.

"We have to head back, brother. Can't stay out here too long and make it a vacation." One of the helicopter crew chiefs said to me over our headsets.

Our visit to the site that nearly took my life was coming to an end. While worth it, my mission wasn't one-hundred percent complete, and there was one thing left for me to prove. I wanted to show the enemy and the place that had taken so much from me that it hadn't defeated me. In the end, I would have the final laugh. So, as the helicopter made its last pass over the over, I did what I felt would be the most symbolic. Instead of remaining seated on board, I disconnected from my seat, grabbed the hand bars on the sides of the open door frame, and stood up.

Look who's still here. Standing mother fuckers! I silently said to myself, symbolically showing the enemy they may have won that battle, but I was here for the long haul. I was back in their backyard, doing exactly what they never intended for me. Surviving and pushing forward, living each day as a better and stronger person than the last.

A WEIGHT LIFTED

Never allow a day to go to waste. Well, that's at least my perspective on life today. I try to view each day with a positive approach and to make it count. This thought process didn't occur overnight. Reading my story in the previous chapters, anyone can see that I once had a different outlook on life. Some days were good, and others were filled with darkness and uncertainty. And once in a while, I simply wanted to give up on life.

Thankfully, today I try to live a different life. One who is positive and uplifting. Not allowing negative thoughts or situations to control who I strive to be. Not just for myself but for those around me. As I've stated before, the road to recovery is long and never truly ends. I still struggle from time to time with my wounds. Although, I don't allow them to take control of me. How we choose to access and react to each struggle matters the most.

Since leaving the army, I've matured a great deal over the years. So much that it's hard to look back at the person I used to be. However, I appreciate the experience and hindsight. At a time in my life, I had a hard time dealing with losing my brothers overseas. While I still mourn their loss and think of them daily, I don't allow it to hinder me as I used to.

Tens of thousands of US troops weren't granted the same fortune as me. Over a dozen of them, I knew personally. Though I was permanently scarred and physically injured, I was given a life to live. Not making the best of the opportunity to make the best of my life is a disservice to those who didn't make it back home.

Getting after the day, accomplishing goals, and enjoying my time here is the least I can do to show my appreciation. They gave their lives so that I could live mine. Given a different set of circumstances, I would have done and expected the same of my brothers.

I survived the IED explosion for a reason. I'm not sure why I lived and others didn't. Nor do I understand the grand scheme of things or my life's purpose. Looking back on that day in Adhamiyah, Iraq, I don't know how I survived. Statistically, I wasn't supposed to. But, I realize that being here today and sharing some of my stories is a miracle. Knowing this makes me want to keep going and make the best of what I have. The further I go; hopefully, I can find and fulfill my purpose along the way.

Besides, what would be the point of staying at home, feeling sorry for myself and the things I can not change? Those days that I waste away, stuck in my mind, are days I'll never get back. If I allowed my circumstances to take control, I couldn't accomplish much of anything in life. Then, as I mature more, sometime in the future, I'll look back and ask myself, what was the purpose of it all? Wasting this precious life, not doing anything, and unable to get that time back.

I used to not have the same approach to life. But, after leaving the hospital and settling into my home, I did the exact opposite. Rather than taking on new adventures, finding new hobbies, and meeting new people, I shied away. I stayed to myself, and the idea of accomplishing something new after the military wasn't a thought.

I spent most of my time being the guy who drank alone or the loner at a dive bar if I chose to go anywhere. The money that I saved, I blew on pointless, meaningless items that I didn't need. I didn't realize it at the time, but I was trying to fill the hole of sadness I had with materialistic objects. Essentially, I was wasting the life I was given a second chance at and allowing meaningful experiences to pass me by.

My negative lifestyle was taking a turn for

the worse. I knew that if I allowed it to continue, it was heading down a path of destruction and regret. I was beginning to gain unhealthy weight, I wasn't getting enough sleep, and I was becoming someone I couldn't stand.

Then, on a random morning during the week, I was awakened by my phone ringing next to my bed. It was an incoming call from Rodney. Someone who I've known over the years and grew to become great friends with. He owned a gym nearby, less than a thirty-minute drive from my house, and hosted various athletic and weight lifting events from time to time. Normally, I would have chosen to sleep and lay in bed until the sun rose. But I hadn't, for some reason, on that particular morning. And I'm glad I decided to answer rather than get back to him through text at a later date.

After finding my contact information, he wanted to formally invite me out to his gym, where he was hosting a strongman competition. An event where some of the strongest men and women would come out for friendly competition. I decided to take him up on the offer and make the trip. I didn't have anything else going on that day, and it would give me an excuse to take my new truck out for a ride. So I got out of bed, cleaned up, and threw on a casual outfit.

I figured there wouldn't be any need for my participation and would only attend to offer my support. If there was going to be any physical exercise or weight lifting involved, I wasn't dressed for the part. I also hadn't planned on doing anything of the sort. It's been years since I've lifted weights or pushed myself physically. Other than small work around my house, I hadn't done much. Because of my injuries, I couldn't do anything too strenuous. Something as easy as walking a block or two with my prosthetic was a workout by itself.

The best shape I've ever been in was during my deployment to Iraq. I had to be if I wanted to succeed and thrive at my job. Carrying fifty seventy pounds of gear or more in the desert heat wasn't a task for the weak. Working out was the only thing to keep you occupied when we were off for the day or not on a mission. Exercising was the perfect remedy if you wanted to keep your mind from losing itself, stuck in a warzone for a year.

Unfortunately, after my injuries, I couldn't possibly keep up with a fitness regimen. I knew that the chances of me lifting weights again were unlikely. Over time, I lost interest in it without the consistency of working out. The physical pain I was constantly in was enough to deal with as it was. Pushing myself to the limit and enduring the pain that comes with working out wasn't something I seemed I would enjoy.

Pulling up to Rodney's new gym, I was greeted by an oversized Strongman banner hanging at the entrance. A few people were standing outside, wearing workout apparel, and carrying gallon-sized water bottles. They appeared in good shape and looked like they knew their way around a weight room. I thought nothing of it and made my way through the front doors.

Heavy metal music played over the gym surround sound speakers, and everything appeared brand new. It was a well-put-together facility, and the smell of sweaty bodies barely filled the air. It reminded me a lot of the gyms on a military base. What appeared to be a couple of dozen people, all carrying positive energy about themselves.

"Dude! Thanks so much for coming out. Glad you could make it." Rodney walked over to me, near the receptionist's table, where I had been standing.

Unlike what I was wearing, Rodney was dressed in shorts, a t-shirt cut at the sleeves, and a pair of workout shoes. He had a light sweat on his forehead and a towel. I knew he had been working out, and his gym wasn't solely reserved for hosting a Strongman competition. By the looks, the comp made up only a portion of what was happening, and everyone was free to work out. Knowing my natural competitive personality, I felt as if I had walked myself right into a trap. It was a room full of men and women who wanted to push themselves, all with competitive and alpha personalities. Highly contagious character traits.

"What's shaking your building, brother? You build this place next to a train station?" I jokingly asked Rodney. The gym floor would vibrate every few seconds, accompanied by a loud, metallic clang. Besides a military-funded gym, this was my first real experience in a professional gym. One with all the bells and whistles in a professional establishment. The vibration that shook the floor was quite intense, and I wasn't sure if there was a problem or if the integrity of his new gym was in jeopardy.

"Bro, those are the Strongman powerlifters. I think they're training for a national competition or something and decided they wanted to use the gym and put on a show for the onlookers. I've known them for some time, and they always find a way to stop in from time to time. It's a pretty chill spot, especially during the week. There aren't a ton of rules that you have to follow to enjoy a good workout. I just want people to be able to come here, feel at home, and train hard." He responded.

After telling me some of the ins and outs of

his gym, he led me over to the powerlifters. He thought the weight those guys could lift was mindblowing and felt I should check it out. They were tucked away in the corner of the gym, towards the back. As I got closer, the vibration on the floor intensified, and I could hear the sound of someone shouting over the music.

I've seen a lot of weights before, and it wasn't something I was unfamiliar with. In the army, I've watched guys stack three forty-five-pound weights on each side of a barbell and bench press it, no problem. And, in my prime, I could easily lift over two-hundred and fifty pounds for at least ten reps. However, the amount of weight these powerlifters were throwing around was incredible. After counting the heavy plates he had stacked on the forty-pound bar, I thought my eyes were playing tricks on me.

I watched one of the powerlifters pick up so much weight that the bar began bending and flexing, forming the shape of a bow. I was honestly impressed and didn't think that he would be able to lift the bar completely off the ground. Once he completed the lift, he released his grip, and the weight that came crashing down felt and sounded like thunder. I had never seen anything like it. These guys were lifting weight as much as an engine block, if not more, and seemed superhuman.

The powerlifters weren't what I would expect someone to look like, capable of lifting the weight they were. They didn't have the appearance of someone as solid as granite, chiseled out of stone, or the icon Arnold Schwarzenegger in his prime. Instead, they were quite average-looking. Someone that, in passing by, you knew they worked out but wouldn't cause you to take a second look.

"Dude, you should give it a try," Rodney suggested.

"You've got to be kidding me, right? There's no way I'm doing that. Look at me."

I wasn't sure if he was joking or not. It didn't take someone with perfect vision to realize I wasn't in shape. Let alone my obvious physical injuries and an amputated leg. There were some things I was comfortable giving a try. However, I had my limitations. Lifting hundreds of pounds off the ground, on a wobbly leg, with hands and fingers fused and limited in motion, spelled failure.

"Nah, man, not that much weight. Hell, I couldn't attempt that on my best day. These guys have been lifting like this for years. We'll take some weight off and let you try it out." Rodney insisted.

No matter how much I tried to avoid lifting, Rodney pressed even harder. I mentioned my hands not being able to properly grab a bar, but that still wasn't enough to get out of it. Finally, he went to a nearby draw and pulled out a pair of cloth weight lifting straps. They were used by weightlifters to allow them to gain a better grip when lifting.

Rodney continued, insisting I step in and give it a shot. With his persistence and the small group of onlookers watching, my ego got the best of me, and I eventually cracked under peer pressure. The powerlifters standing around the barbell were excited to see my participation and began removing some of the weight. I expected them to replace the larger plates with smaller ones or bring the weight to a reasonable amount. I was wrong. They removed a couple of plates on each side and called me over for an attempt.

Four hundred and five pounds were left on the bar. Over one hundred pounds heavier than the most I had ever lifted. I was honestly nervous and didn't want to embarrass myself. But it was too late to back out now. Rodney placed the straps around my wrist and helped me use them to gain a better grip around the bar. The guys were standing around, beginning to cheer me on and giving me words of encouragement.

Maybe they know something I don't know. I said to myself. I wondered if everyone looking on saw something in me that I hadn't. Or this was an average amount of weight. Perhaps I had been away from working out so long that four hundred pounds was a moderate lift.

"Let's go!" One of the lifters shouted from beside me.

Stepping up on a small platform, I bent over

and placed both hands around the bar as best as possible. Despite using the straps, I would still have to use considerable strength to prevent the weight from slipping from my grasp. This wasn't like the bench press, which I was familiar with. Instead, the type of lift I would perform was the deadlift. A form of lifting requiring the individual to stand. Rather than lay flat on a bench, press the weight off and away from them.

I took a deep breath and focused, putting all my attention on not messing this up or embarrassing myself. Then, pulling up as hard as I could, the four-hundred-pound weight lifted off the ground. Surprisingly, much easier than I expected, and I didn't feel I was using all of my strength. But, for a moment, I questioned the validity of the lift. I thought that somehow, some of the weights were styrofoam props, used in some elaborate prank against me.

"Bro! That's what I'm talking about!" Rodney shouted, accompanied by words of praise from those standing by.

The energy that filled the room around me was a feeling I'd felt before. It was the same energetic vibe I would get surrounded by my brothers in arms, all focused on one common goal. A feeling that I had missed and longed for. However, I couldn't find it anywhere outside of the military.

It honestly felt good knowing I hadn't lost all my strength. Better than I expected it to be. I wasn't sure how the lift would play out, but I'm glad it went the way it had. It would be the first time I had ever completed a deadlift. Of course, I know it wasn't in proper form, and I resembled nothing like the powerlifters. But, nonetheless, I was more than satisfied with what I had achieved.

After a few handshakes, pats on the back, and congratulations, Rodney suggested I make the trip more often. There wouldn't be a gym membership fee or sign up for any classes unless I wanted to. He only asked that I show up and see where it would take me. If anything, it would get me out of the house and give me something else to do to fill my free time. I usually had no plans during the mornings, so I figured I would take him up on his offer.

Rodney's gym was open every day of the week, Monday through Saturday. Each day had a workout routine in one of the classes, focussing on a particular muscle group. The day that I attended was a Wednesday. A day dedicated to deadlifts and squats. One of the most dreaded workout days in the gym due to the heavy lifting and soreness it carries with it.

I returned the following days, exercising each day for about an hour. I wanted to ease myself back into the lifestyle rather than jump in feet first. Plus, taking my time to better get acquainted with my limitations. I needed to know what I was capable of doing and what I couldn't so I wouldn't hurt myself.

Each day I showed up to his gym was better than the previous one. Slowly but surely, I started to feel my strength again. I didn't realize how much I missed working out and how it benefited me. Not only physically but mentally as well. Having something as simple as lifting something and placing it back down requires more focus and determination than you would expect.

I was officially bitten by the iron bug. A term describing a novice practitioner addicted to lifting within the gym community. I looked forward to waking up in the mornings and heading to the gym to train. I have thought about it every day since my first stepping into Rodney's facility. It was the only thing at that time that kept my mind from wandering too far into my past military experiences and trauma.

The following week, Wednesday was deadlift day again. But, this time, I came prepared. Earlier in the week, I purchased a cheap pair of lifting straps and comfortable attire. The powerlifters were there as well and excited to see that I showed up to work out with them. After a brief warmup, one of the lifters suggested that I try to break my previous gym record of four hundred and five pounds with a heavier lift.

Before stacking forty-pound plates onto the bar, the guys showed me a few trade tricks I could use to help me out. The first two large plates were added, followed by four, six, eight, and ten. My eyes grew wide as I watched them search for more weight to place on the bar. Finally, after surpassing the four hundred pounds I originally managed to lift, twelve plates were stacked against each other on the bar. Six secured on each side.

Five hundred and forty pounds, not including the weight of the barbell, lay on the floor in front of me.

"It ain't going to lift itself, brother. You got this. Four hundred was paperweight for you. This is no problem." One of the powerlifters assured.

I wouldn't have believed you if you told me I would be attempting to lift something heavier than a Blue Whale's heart a month ago. However, that was the task at hand today, and I wasn't going to let it intimidate me or back away from the challenge.

After getting my straps situated around my

wrists and onto the bar and using the powerlifters' advice, I tugged and pulled until I stood upright.

Holy shit! I said to myself. I was in shock at what had taken place. But, even more so, getting the weight off the ground wasn't as hard as I thought it would be. In fact, it was almost too easy.

"Dude! Do you know what you just did?" Looking on from the opposite side of the gym, Rodney congratulated me.

"It didn't feel like it was too much weight at all. Is it a big deal or what?" I asked.

"Listen, I've been around and trained people who can lift heavy for years now. But, what you just did, is something that isn't an easy task by far. There aren't many people out there who can just walk into a gym and, a week later, deadlift over five hundred pounds." Rodney continued.

I think I was as shocked as everyone else. It wasn't as challenging as I thought it would be, and I could have lifted more.

I continued to show up almost every day at Rodney's gym for months. Each day, I pushed myself harder and harder, setting new goals and accomplishing them. It didn't take long for me to fall in love with the hobby. Lifting weights became a part of my life, and I thoroughly enjoyed it. I became addicted to the thrill and rush of it. Other than the rush I got in combat, the dose of adrenaline I received lifting was something I hadn't felt in a long time.

Powerlifting and working out gave me what I needed and was missing in my life. Something that I haven't found since serving in the army. The military was the only thing that provided me with structure and discipline. In the army, a specific training regimen must be followed with extreme dedication to being an effective soldier, especially as a warfighter. Weightlifting provided all of these traits. And the camaraderie that came along with lifting at the gym was hard to come by. Sticking to my newfound hobby was the closest feeling I would get to being back with my guys in an infantry squad.

In the beginning, I didn't know where weightlifting would take me. If anywhere at all. I saw it as simply doing something that I loved. However, after months and months of training, Rodney and the group of powerlifters I trained with suggested that I go professional. Before then, I never knew that such a thing as professional powerlifting existed. Let alone that I was good enough, they would recommend I should try it out. The only thing I wanted to accomplish at the professional level was football. After my injuries, I never considered taking anything to such a high level. I was under the impression that my dreams of accomplishing anything that involved physical activity as a professional were over.

After giving the idea, Rodney and the guys gave me some thought; I figured, why not? I already proved that I wasn't going to make a fool of myself and could do it. So I took my training to the next level each gym session. Each day, pushing myself more and more. Dialing in and perfecting my technique.

I asked as many questions as possible from guys much stronger than me and took what they offered to heart. If I was going to do this, I wanted to ensure I did it right. There wasn't going half throttle in weightlifting. It was either all or nothing.

Later, the following year, I found myself in the entertainment capital of the world, Las Vegas, Nevada. A professional weightlifting show was underway, and I would be competing in it. It was a surreal moment in my life. I still had difficulty comprehending that something that began on a random morning would place me here. Yet, here I was, grateful for the invite Rodney gave me to attend his gym and train.

The competition gathered hundreds of competitors from all over the world. To be amongst them was an experience I couldn't have dreamed of, to say the least. I would compete in the paralympic category, performing the bench press and deadlift against other individuals with various disabilities. While my injuries were unique, I knew I could hold my own.

"Next up, we have Omar Avila!" The announcer's voice over a loudspeaker introduced me to the stage. Hearing my name called out in the setting, I was in was a moment I'll never forget.

As I made my way to the center of the platform on stage, an Olympic barbell with multiple plates on each side awaited me. In total, over six hundred and seventy-five pounds, and this was my third and final lift.

Competing, we were allotted three lifts. The first is what we knew we could achieve. The second attempt was for our personal records in the gym. And the third was reserved for the most weight we'd ever attempt.

Reaching down and grabbing the bar, I looked out at the crowd in front of me. A sea of people were watching me as I attempted to make the lift. It was a humbling experience. Not only was I representing myself and those who helped me get to this point, but I also represented my brothers in arms.

I wanted to make the guys who never made it back home proud and the countless soldiers who returned with missing limbs and scars they'll have forever. I wanted them to look at what I was able to accomplish, despite my injuries and wounds and all that I've been through, and know that they could achieve more. I didn't see myself as anyone special or better than anyone else. But I knew that if I could make it this far, anyone could.

I took a breath, relaxed my nerves, and focused on the task. Reaching down and wrapping the straps around the bar, I gripped as tightly as possible. I couldn't afford to have any hiccups and wanted this deadlift to be flawless. A group of powerlifters stood around me, cheering me on and acting as spotters in case the weight was too much for me to handle. Finally, one standing to my side slapped me on my shoulder and snapped me into my zone.

Go time! I whispered, gritting my teeth to prepare for the lift.

"Clear! Lift complete!" The next thing I remembered was hearing the announcer's voice. I had been so tuned in and focused that I hadn't realized that my lift was already over. It was nearly a perfect deadlift execution, weighing almost seven hundred pounds.

The rush that took over me is one hard to articulate or give justice to. So riveting. I remember dropping the weight to the sounds of a crowd screaming and applauding. I was so excited that I screamed at the top of my lungs, balling my fists up as hard as possible. I felt unstoppable. Damn near bulletproof at that moment. Besides joining the army, it was one of the greatest moments I've had the opportunity to experience.

It was official. I was a weightlifting world record holder, and my family's last name was attached. I went on to continue to compete and broke additional records in the bench press as well as deadlift. To say that I'm still shocked to hold such a title would be false. Although, it's a title I couldn't be more proud to have.

There's a drastic difference between someone who struggled and fought with himself to get out of bed to where I am today. And I'm thankful I chose to stay along for the ride, regardless of what happened in my past. If there's a lesson I've learned, it's to never give up. Instead, try to take each day we have alive and make the best of it. Sure, it's going to suck and get bumpy along the way, but keep driving. You'll be surprised by all the great things ahead that you never before believed possible.

The only question that I ask now is, what's next? Whatever it is, I know I will be enjoying the ride.

Omar "Crispy" Avila

ABOUT THE AUTHOR

Omar Avila has had a life of service dedicated to his country and his fellow veterans. Avila joined the U.S. Army in 2004 as an Infantryman, deploying to Iraq in 2006. On May 14, 2006, his vehicle was struck with a 200 lb IED, resulting in burns to 75% of his body and amputation below the knee of his right leg. Upon retiring from the U.S. Army in 2010, Avila never allowed his injuries to slow his success. Powering through his injuries, he became the current world record holder for the World Association of Bench and Deadlift in the Paralympics category. Avila now serves to motivate wounded veterans, seeks to educate the public about veteran issues through numerous public speaking events, and is a sought-after motivational speaker. A lifelong avid hunter, Omar also spreads his passion for the outdoors by assisting wounded veterans. Avila was raised in Brownsville, TX and currently lives in New Braunfels, TX.